Enjoy!
Irene Pollin

IRENE AND ABE

AN UNEXPECTED LIFE

By

Irene Pollin

www.irenepollin.com

ISBN: 978-0-692-62123-3

Printed by:
Artisan II
4311 Wheeler Avenue
Alexandria, VA 22304
(703) 823-4636
www.artisan2inc.com

Book layout by:
Debra Brunner
Custom Designers, Inc.
12914 Fitzwater Drive
Nokesville, VA 20181
(703) 594-3125
www.customdesigners.com

Cover design by:
Grafik
625 North Washington Street
Suite 302
Alexandria, VA 22314
www.grafik.com

Published by:
Irene Pollin
4701 Willard Avenue
Suite 223
Chevy Chase, MD 20815-4609
(301) 986-1201

ACKNOWLEDGMENTS

Dear Reader,

As I finish this book after four years of unexpected ups and downs and consider whom to thank for helping with this difficult but satisfying project, I come up with only a few names. The reason is that I didn't seek help from a lot of people. Mostly, I felt I needed to work out the problems myself. After all, it is a personal story.

But there were several people whose support, assistance and love helped me along this journey.

Two women helped me organize the facts of my life: Linda Cashdan and Salley Shannon. Linda was the first who took ninety years of a varied, full and public life and created a workable draft. Salley took the draft and helped bring it to life. How many hours did we sit and cry and laugh?

Elaine Gill, my assistant, took a box of assorted photos—personal and public—and gave them order.

Without these women, I'd have given up long ago. Thanks and hugs!

Next, there were a number of friends who were willing to fill in some of my thinking on personal relationships. You know who you are!

During the process of writing my book, I was reminded of how grateful I am to my parents, Goldie and Herman Kerchek, who gave me everything I needed to get through life.

And, I want to thank my "can count on" family: my beloved niece Ilene Ellenbogen, who never lets me down.

Finally, my children: my son Jimmy, who is there when I need him and even more; and my son Robert and his wife Sigrid, whose idea this was in the first place. This began as a birthday gift from them and became the most important journey of my life.

Although the title of the book is *An Unexpected Life*, the experience of writing it was even more unexpected. Thank you, with love.

Two roads diverged in a yellow wood,
And sorry I could not travel both
And be one traveler, long I stood
And looked down one as far as I could
To where it bent in the undergrowth;

Then took the other, as just as fair,
And having perhaps the better claim,
Because it was grassy and wanted wear;
Though as for that the passing there
Had worn them really about the same,

And both that morning equally lay
In leaves no step had trodden black.
Oh, I kept the first for another day!
Yet knowing how way leads on to way,
I doubted if I should ever come back.

I shall be telling this with a sigh
Somewhere ages and ages hence:
Two roads diverged in a wood, and I—
I took the one less traveled by,
And that has made all the difference.

"The Road Not Taken"– Robert Frost

We look before and after,
And pine for what is not:
Our sincerest laughter
With some pain is fraught;
Our sweetest songs are those that tell of saddest thought.

From "To a Skylark"– Percy Bysshe Shelley

Don't go where the path may lead, go instead where
there is no path…and leave a trail.

– Unknown

This book is dedicated to my parents,

Goldie and Herman Kerchek.

PROLOGUE

Imagine you are sitting with me on my porch. I am wearing my favorite black and white striped knit top from L.L. Bean and my Eileen Fisher black cotton pants. It's three in the afternoon and the light is beginning to soften as I offer you some tea and chocolate chip cookies. You came over at my invitation to hear stories of my life. You are interested because some aspects of it are unusual. And I am perfectly happy to tell my stories—funny, sad, short, long, painful, even upsetting. Normally, as a psychotherapist, I am the listener. Now the role is reversed. But, I am eager to share my stories, because working on the book has opened doors long closed and created connections never before made.

CHAPTER ONE

As luck would have it, our first away game as owners of the Baltimore Bullets took place in St. Louis, my hometown. We invited my whole family, lots of cousins of all ages, and we all cheered so loudly that one woman sitting in front of us finally turned around and said, "Why are you yelling like that for the Bullets? You'd think you owned the team!" Abe loved to tell that story along with several other stories from that weekend because the game coincided with the first meeting we attended, also in St. Louis, of owners of National Basketball Association league teams. My cousins still talk about it. "Remember the time Irene brought Boston Celtics owner Red Auerbach to our house for lunch?"

There were Abe and I—the new kids on the block—mixing with basketball legends we had up to that time only read about. While Red Auerbach was explaining to me how his favorite trick was to turn up the heat in the visiting team's locker room in Boston to tire the guys out before the game started, Abe was across the room chatting strategy with Knicks founder and basketball icon Ned Irish (who had just been inducted into the Basketball Hall of Fame) and giving me a look that said *I can't believe I'm talking to Ned Irish!*

It was a very heady experience for us, suddenly finding ourselves on the inside, listening to the behind-the-scenes talk about coaches and players and strategy and trades.

"Irene, have you met Wilt Chamberlain?" someone asked me. As I turned to shake Chamberlain's hand, I found my eyes at the exact same level as the over-seven-foot-tall player's belly button. He seemed to me to be a living statue. I had never seen a live person that big. He just didn't seem real. And there I was talking to him.

It was at that point that I found myself asking: *How in the world did I ever (ever!) end up in the world of professional basketball?*

=============

It may seem strange to love going to a cemetery. But, I cherish my visits to one in St. Louis because I always feel I'm going there to relive fond memories and "visit" people I loved very much. Two women buried there—my aunt and my grandmother—were very special to me. Their tombstones face each other. When I stand between the two, I feel the warmth and love they showered on me as a child.

An uncle purchased a section of the cemetery just for our large family, the Orensteins. As I look at the names on each of the smaller stones, I felt the bond of family that is missing today.

My maternal grandparents, Shifra Rimel and Chaim Shika Goren, married in Russia and moved to St. Louis before my time. They were my forebears. My grandfather and his children immigrated to the United States. My grandmother, my mother Goldie and her younger sister Fanny joined them in St. Louis around 1916. My cousin Fern remembers my mother and her sister at the time of their arrival as two very pretty teenagers who wore colorful, elaborate Russian dresses.

My father, Herman "Gersh" Kirchik, (the spelling of his name changed to Kerchek when he moved from Russia) followed my mother to St. Louis. According to his sister Bobtse, Herman's good looks, charm and skill at dancing made him extremely popular with the girls in Zaslav, Russia. But, once he met Goldie, that was it. Following Goldie to the United States could not have been an easy decision for him. It meant leaving behind his mother and sister—uncertain he would ever see them again—as well as a successful family hotel business. But, he was in love.

Unfortunately, he decided to follow Goldie at a time when U.S. immigration laws had become restrictive. Unable to enter the country, he spent a year in Cuba, where he was persuasive enough to talk someone into letting him sell ties on the street. He did so well that he contemplated having my mother join him there. The idea was quite tempting, she told me later, but she did not want to leave her relatives. He met her in St. Louis instead, and they never regretted it. She had a wonderful, warm family which took my father in as one of its own. I've always loved the romance of his pursuit, and have kept, all these years, a card he sent my mother from Cuba in 1916 with his picture and a love poem he'd written to her in Russian. The translation:

> *The goal of my life is to love you. It's not in*
> *my power to forget you.*
> *If you love me the way I love you,*
> *We should be friends forever.*
> *To Charming Golda with kind regards from*
> *Gersh Kirchik.*

Those feelings never changed. My father was very affectionate and showed it. He absolutely adored my mother every day of their married life. They did battle occasionally, like all married couples, but it never lasted. He always gave in to her stronger will.

My parents spoke a lot about their lives in Russia, and although my mother did talk of being afraid enough to run and hide when the Cossacks came racing their horses through the main street of her town of Triesk, she always described her childhood in positive ways. Triesk, she said, was a pretty village with a river running through the center, surrounded by thick green forests, where as a young tomboy she loved climbing trees.

Given the period in which they grew up, both of my parents were well-educated. My mother's father was a rabbi and both my mother and my grandmother were unusually literate for women in that period. I have wonderful memories of my grandmother Shifra sitting at my Aunt Bertha's kitchen table reading a huge Torah. My mother had read all the great Russian novelists, which she introduced to me and later to my husband. Recently, my son Robert found a book she had given Abe, *War and Peace*, inscribed to her "future son-in-law." Education was highly valued in my family.

By the time my mother arrived in St. Louis, the Orensteins were well-established. Her father's brothers had successful businesses and were active in the community. I remember how proud I was on the High Holy Days, going to the synagogue with my grandmother and being greeted by all her elegant, white-haired and white-bearded brothers. They were all presidents of their synagogues. She was their only sister.

Soon after my father came to the United States, my parents married. I was born in 1924; my sister, Betty, six years later. We were a small family nestled in the bosom of a larger one, since my mother's sister, Aunt Bertha, Uncle Joe and their four daughters lived only a few blocks away. The two households were interchangeable. My sister and I loved being in their home. We spent as much time in their home as we did at our own. I loved stopping by Aunt Bertha's on my way home from school, and whenever I had a fight or disagreement with my mother, I knew I could get sympathy and hugs from my aunt and grandmother. They always explained why my mother yelled at me and said how much she loved me. This helped me to understand my mother, who did have a quick temper.

Even though my father was well educated and had come from a comfortable hotel business in Russia, to provide for his young family he had to take a job with the Pevely Dairy Company, delivering heavy metal containers of milk in a horse drawn carriage at 3 a.m. After a few years when he finished his runs, he'd join my mother in the grocery store they operated. My Uncle Joe was a tailor and Aunt Bertha operated a dry goods business out of their apartment. All my adult family members did whatever work was necessary to maintain their families.

The glue that held the family together was my grandmother, Shifra, who lived with Bertha. Shifra was tiny—five feet at most— and by the age of ten, I towered over her. But what she lacked in physical stature, she made up for in emotional force. She was quiet, soft spoken, and unobtrusive, but with a strength of character that prevailed. She was our protector. If we did something wrong and our parents came after us, she would stand in front of us and spread out her apron, shielding us from their wrath.

She was also our mediator. Whenever there was a fight among the cousins (and there were many!), she managed to bring us back together. Imagine this tiny woman, joining the hands of the two cousins who were pushing and shoving each other, and forcing them to pull together. Of course, we resisted. But she never gave up until we could all laugh together about the disagreement, kiss, and make up. She called this process "ahver shaver." I always assumed "ahver shaver" was a Russian expression or an ancient tradition between Jewish grandmothers and their grandchildren. Since I have never been able to find one other grandmother who used "ahver shaver," I have no idea whether the words are translatable or exist in any language. But I love the concept.

When I was sick with various childhood diseases, a special treat was my grandmother sitting by my bed and telling me story after story. She knew all the Sholem Aleichem stories and had many of her own. "But I just told you that one!" she would say, and I would tell her I didn't care. I wanted to hear it again. Often they were funny or even a bit raunchy, and sometimes sad. I'll never forget the true story she told of why she walked with a slight sway. She had been riding in an open wagon in Russia one bitterly cold day as a child, and her feet froze, and she lost the use of her toes.

She was very forthcoming and answered all my questions. When I asked her why she wore a wig (a funny-looking one), she explained it was the Orthodox tradition that when she married she had to cover her hair. I once asked her to remove it so I could see the thin, grayish hair underneath. I loved to listen to stories about her life in Russia.

Just as some generations remember vividly where they were when Kennedy died, my cousins and I remember vividly where we were on Saturday, June 26, 1937—the day my grandmother died. I was in a movie theater when one of my cousins rushed into the dark theater crying, "Baba's dying, Baba's dying." I grabbed my sister's hand and ran to the bus stop. I remember sitting in the back, looking out of the window at the pouring rain and thinking, "God is angry that she's dying." When we got to the hospital, I knew children were not allowed to go to her floor, so I avoided the elevator and ran up the stairs. When I burst into the room, my aunts and mother couldn't believe how I, a thirteen-year-old with a seven-year-old in tow, had made it without being seen. Nothing would stop me from seeing my precious Baba before she died.

There is not a day, even today, when I do not think of my grandmother and the unconditional, absolute love she imparted to all of her grandchildren, a love exemplified by the fact that each of us was certain she alone was my grandmother's favorite.

One of the many stories I loved to hear was how my grandmother's marriage was arranged. I couldn't imagine that. Had she known him before? How did she feel? She told me she had eventually grown to love him, even though he had a quick temper (to go with his red hair). In fact, she told me, it was his temper that killed him. One evening after dinner he became so angry that he had a heart attack and died immediately. At the time, my mother was pregnant with me, and so I was named after him. "Irene Sue" was the English translation of the Yiddish feminine translation of Chaim Shika.

In addition to the name, I think I inherited his quick temper, which I learned to control over time. I've often wondered whether his love of learning was passed down to me genetically as well. As a child I loved school and excelled academically. I skipped two grades and graduated top in my class from elementary school, which went to the eighth grade, and finished high school at the age of sixteen. I was always two years ahead of my peers, the youngest but also the tallest. I never went to camp in the summer or even on trips with my family; we couldn't afford it. Instead I spent my summers reading and going to baseball games. (Both activities would influence my later life.) I used to walk almost every day to the local library. This was before air-conditioning, and the library was wonderfully dark and cool. I'd always come home with my arms full of books. My favorites were a series featuring twins from different countries—Chinese twins, Spanish twins, Irish twins, Dutch twins, Eskimo twins, and so on—which created my passion for travel that would continue throughout my life. I was fascinated by the different cultures and languages the series described and longed to visit all of the countries one day.

I read everything, and the books I found greatly enhanced my world. At age twelve, I had not yet seen a ballet, so reading about the life of Ukrainian-born dancer Vaslav Nijinsky—famous for his grandiose leaps and creative choreography—was fascinating, exciting. Another book I read, *Jews Without Money*, shocked me with its graphic descriptions and black and white drawings of life in a Jewish ghetto. The book was written in 1930 by Michael Gold, and described life in the Jewish ghetto of New York City as a nightmarish mixture of prostitutes, sweatshops, howling pushcart peddlers, and scary rat-infested tenements that had "bedbugs bloated with blood." One photo of a prostitute being fondled on the steps of a brownstone still haunts me. The vivid descriptions were shocking for a twelve-year-old, especially a protected Jewish twelve-year-old, and a dramatic contrast to the world I knew.

The St. Louis I grew up in was filled with first-rate cultural institutions. We had a superb art museum, an excellent symphony orchestra, and the delightful Muny Opera that performed in the park during the summer. My parents loved music, especially opera, and we were at the park on blankets listening to music at least once a week. We lived in a predominantly Jewish neighborhood, but nothing like the ghetto described in the book. I lived in buildings surrounded by grass and trees and lots of space, and the schools were good. We had parks we could walk to, and we did. I remember my mother's older sister, Aunt Irene, saying that she would never live in a city where there were no parks.

In 1941, I graduated from University City High School. I felt on top of the world at that stage in my life—smart, confident, excited about the future, and pretty, too. I had suddenly started attracting the opposite sex, and here I was sixteen years old dating guys in their twenties; some in college, some even older who were already in business. One day in broad daylight when one of those "older men" drove up to my house in a shiny red convertible with the top down, I stood outside hanging on to the door for a while so all the neighbors could see. The summer was looking promising.

Because they were older, they took me dancing at the Chase Hotel in St. Louis. It was exciting and glamorous. In retrospect, I think I was psychologically a very young sixteen, and part of my confidence came from a lack of sophistication. I couldn't wait to get out there, but I had no idea what the rest of the world was like. I had no plans, but lots of hopes. I felt I was looking into a future where anything was possible. I planned to attend Washington University at some point, but I had time. Bolstered by the solid nurturing I'd received from my family and the academic success I'd enjoyed, I felt the whole world was open to me. Why, for the first time in my life, I was going to travel on my own outside St. Louis! I was on my way to the nation's capital, Washington, D.C.

My mother's sister, Fanny, was married to a man named Dan Pollin. I knew them from their family visits to St. Louis. Aunt Fanny had been inviting me for several years, and I was going to spend the summer with them in Washington, D.C.

In 1941 the train ride from St. Louis to Washington took eighteen hours. I sat up all night long, staring out at the sweeping panorama of country I was seeing for the first time, city after city; names that I had only seen on maps or read about in books. So many times had I heard them announce on the radio, "Tonight, Benny Goodman, coming to you from the Steel Pier in Atlantic City!" and now I was going to the East Coast, the place where the popular big bands I'd heard on the radio—Tommy Dorsey and musicians like Artie Shaw and Benny Goodman—actually played. I had no idea where Atlantic City was; all I knew was that those big bands and musicians never played in St. Louis. My adrenaline pumped steadily every minute of that long train ride. I was thrilled.

This trip was taking me to places, physical and emotional, that were completely new. This was the beginning of the rest of my life! It was the overly dramatic certainty of a naïve teenager, but it actually turned out to be true.

=============

Ironically, totally oblivious to the fears generated by my reading *Jews Without Money*, my Aunt Fanny decided to celebrate my arrival by planning a special trip for the two of us to…New York City! We spent the first night at the apartment of cousins; cousins who happened to live on Henry Street in the exact neighborhood described in *Jews Without Money*. I still remember how I felt as I walked up the creaking, narrow stairway to the second floor, and it dawned on me that I was entering a real live tenement just like the ones that I had read about. I slept that night on a cot with some kind of paper under the mattress that made a crunchy noise every time I moved, and I remembered from the book that paper was used to keep the bed bugs from biting. This was exactly what was described in the book, but I never expected to experience it.

A few weeks later, my aunt and I took another trip, this one to visit her son, Jerry, at a summer camp just outside of Philadelphia. Before I came to Washington, my aunt had been telling me that she had a lot of good-looking nephews she was going to introduce me to. I listened politely. The truth was, I was more interested in seeing new places and being away from home and on my own for the first time than I was in meeting boys. Dating was something I could do—and had been doing—in St. Louis. On this trip, sightseeing was a higher priority for me. But, of course as her guest, I agreed to go.

The Pollins, I discovered, were a big family, and several of my aunt's Pollin nephews were there. Arrangements were made for the camp visitors to stay overnight, but there weren't enough beds for all of us. My aunt told me I would be sharing a bed with her sister-in-law, Jenny Pollin, who was visiting her son Harold at the camp.

It was a night that I will never forget for several reasons. First, it turned out to be extremely uncomfortable, because it was very cold and Jenny kept pulling all the blankets off me to cover herself. I was not only cold; I was shocked. I was accustomed to being a nurtured child among caring adults; my parents and aunts would cover the children first. What kind of adult pulls the blankets off a seventeen-year-old kid? I kept wondering, *What type of person is this?*

I would later learn. At the time, how was I to know that one day this woman would become my mother-in-law?

Several of the Pollin nephews Aunt Fanny had been discussing showed up at the camp the next day, and one made sure he stood out. His name was Abe Pollin. He was Jenny's son and Harold's brother, and he was good looking—tall, thin, and athletic with curly blond hair, big blue eyes, and a turned-up nose. His uncle Dan was Aunt Fanny's husband (I called him Uncle Dave). Abe was seventeen, and just happened to stop by on his way home from Atlantic City with a group of his friends. I didn't pay much attention to him at first—there were so many boys around—but he cleverly got me away from the rest of them.

"Come watch me play ping-pong," he urged. "I'm very good—Jewish Community Center Champion." And so I watched as he easily beat opponents, smoothly slamming the ball over the net again and again. I also noticed as I watched that he was also watching my reaction out of the corner of his eye.

I was impressed. He was right. He was an excellent ping-pong player. He was also cute. There was something about him that made him stand out.

Abe returned to Washington at about the same time that my aunt and I did and began taking me around town. This was 1941, the summer before we entered World War II, and Washington was a bit of a backwater town—more like a small southern town than the cosmopolitan national capital I had anticipated. *Is this it???* I wondered when we walked through the National Gallery, which at the time had very few paintings and was not half as impressive as the art museum in St. Louis. The universities in the nation's capital were nothing compared to Washington University in St. Louis. There was only one theater, the National Theatre. I soon discovered the differences between the two cities. This was a government city rather than a commercial center. There were very few private businesses and the only big ones were companies doing construction—the business Abe's father was in.

There were, however, many beautiful national monuments to visit. Abe showed them all to me, along with his prowess at sports other than ping-pong. He was very athletic and enjoyed impressing me. One day he asked me if I could play tennis, and I said yes. I had hit a few balls around, but I didn't realize at the time that "being able to play tennis" required more skill than that. I had no idea how well he played. He took me to a tennis court in Rock Creek

Park, anticipating a solid match, but soon realized that I was not holding up my end of the game. Years later when we talked about that experience, he said the best part about that game was the tight, green-and-white-striped T-shirt I wore.

He was cocky about his athletic prowess. But when he wasn't showing off his skills, he was quite shy, and I was just as shy. Cars didn't have the front-seat separations then that they have today. "May I hold your hand?" he asked one night as I was sitting on the other side of the car. *Is he kidding?* I wondered. I had been dating boys who did not ask permission.

That moment marked the beginning, however—the beginning of my moving closer across the seat, and the beginning of a very long tradition of hand holding, through good times and bad.

There was another significant moment that summer. One night after coming home from a movie with some of his friends, he walked me up to my aunt's front door, took me in his arms and he kissed me. *Really* kissed me. I had never been kissed before by any boy. I'd dated. I'd gone dancing. I'd gone to parties. But, I'd never allowed any date to kiss me except on the cheek. Wow, I thought to myself, so this is what everybody talks about! And while we were standing in the dark outside of my aunt's front door, kissing, I wondered what his three friends were thinking—the friends he'd left back in the car.

The two of us spent the rest of my Washington trip together, not only dating, but spending hours on the telephone when we were apart, talking, talking, talking. I can't think of what we had to talk so much about, but we never ran out of words.

What did we see in each other? Opposites attract and we were quite opposite. I think he was attracted to my self-confidence (and maybe the green and white T-shirt). I was attracted to his looks, his dancing ability, but mostly his calm, thoughtful, safe, gentle manner. It complemented my excitable personality, my readiness to take on risks, challenges. I was very sure of myself, almost downright cocky.

Abe lacked that kind of confidence. He had an older brother he had to compete with all his life, a brother who was outgoing while Abe was shy; talented with his hands, while Abe was clumsy; a brother who was always telling jokes and demanding attention. But Abe was his mother's favorite, which brought with it the embarrassment of being constantly praised. "My Abe is the most brilliant, the most." He was a better student than his older brother and a very good athlete, but his brother dominated when they were in a room together.

I loved Abe's seriousness. He might have been the youngest boy I'd dated, but he was the most mature. He was focused. He was a planner. I did not have plans. I was living day-to-day. I was a bit flighty back then, and he grounded me. I liked that.

Abe's father, Morris Pollin, had come to this country from Russia at fourteen. He was poor, not formally educated, but naturally talented and already a skilled plumber. By the time I met Abe, Morris Pollin owned the largest plumbing and heating company in Washington, D.C. with hundreds of employees. He was a remarkable man. He was extraordinarily generous. I think he felt he had been blessed with good fortune and that developed in him a strong sense of giving back, out of gratitude, whether that meant donating money to Israel or other Jewish causes or setting up his relatives—and their relatives—in business. He wasn't the oldest of the six brothers who had come to America, but he was the one who helped everybody out, whether it was his side of the family or his wife's. He made it possible for many of them to have a decent life.

After coming to Washington in 1931, Morris Pollin had done extraordinarily well financially; he built a fabulous house for his family on a few acres of land at 16th and Colorado, across from Rock Creek Park. The house had a graceful, winding stairway off a beautiful center hall. To the left were a luxurious wood-paneled library and a handsome living room that had been professionally decorated by Washington's leading decorator. The first time Abe took me there I was impressed when a white-jacketed butler opened the door. Standing behind him was Abe's mother, wearing a printed housedress and apron. Jenny Pollin was cleaning with the butler! I believe my mother-in-law never became comfortable with the resources that were now hers.

Morris, on the other hand, loved it. His clothes were beautifully tailored and he proudly drove a LaSalle, which at the time had greater status than a Cadillac. He was a handsome man with a great physique, which he took pride in. He exercised every single morning for an hour, swam, ate vegetables before it was popular to do so, and went to the Jewish Community Center gym regularly. He read *Your Health*, the health version of *Reader's Digest*, like a Bible. He also loved travel and took violin lessons, even though he had a tin ear. He thoroughly enjoyed all of the benefits that his newly acquired wealth allowed him.

Abe was working for his father that summer to learn the business he would run some day with his brother. That meant learning from the bottom up: fixing pipes and even carrying sinks and bathtubs, if necessary. The experienced workers liked to tease him that, because he was such a skinny kid and as "the boss's son," he had it easy on the job.

"Go get a bucket of steam!" they'd laugh. But this only made him more determined to prove he could do anything they could do. One day he carried a bathtub that probably weighed as much as he did (130 pounds) and ended up rupturing several discs in his back, an injury which would later keep him out of military service during the war. This incident stayed with him for the rest of his life because not only did he feel guilty about not having served in the Army, he suffered from back trouble forever.

When I returned to St. Louis at summer's end, he wrote to me every day. I was pleased and flattered. Soon in his letters he was suggesting that he come visit me in St. Louis that Christmas. He did not say, "Can I come?" He said, "I'm coming." I didn't know it at the time, but his mother told him "If you're going all the way to St. Louis to visit a girl, this is serious."

And my mother said, "If he's coming all the way here to see you, this is serious." I had no idea what that meant.

Then, on December 7, Pearl Harbor happened and soldiers began heading to training camps and overseas. I didn't think he would come. After all, the world had changed since our summer fun.

Abe not only showed up as he said he would, but he brought me an incredible gift: a portable radio. In those days, a portable radio was barely portable. It was huge and heavy, but I was so awed by the gift I lugged that thing around so all my friends could see it.

I met him at the train station, an odd figure among all the soldiers in uniform. He had been standing in the aisle or sitting on his suitcase the whole eighteen hours. This was one determined guy. I still didn't understand what it all meant, but I have to admit I was extremely flattered.

My mother had made arrangements for him to stay in a small hotel near our apartment, but when she saw the hotel room she decided that it would not do. After all, this was her sister's nephew. She quickly made arrangements for him to sleep on a cot in our apartment. While she was making all these arrangements, I think she was going back and forth mentally, keenly aware of his seriousness. On one hand, she knew good things about the Pollin family, but on the other she kept saying, "He's so young."

He was young, but he was fun to be with. More important, there was a very interesting, serious side to him—the talking side. "Mother, he's very mature," I told her. And he *was* mature. How else could he have followed through on all the decisions he made? He thought and planned so carefully. We had a wonderful time together, dancing at night and seeing St. Louis during the day. I was quite proud of my city. The Saint Louis Art Museum in Forest Park, which was also next to Washington University where I one day planned to attend, was one of my favorite places. I also couldn't wait to introduce him to my all my friends—boys and girls—who, however, were not that enthusiastic, especially the boys. Who was this interloper? I was so naïve.

It wasn't long after the Christmas visit before he began writing to me every day again, but this time suggesting I move to Washington. (Where did he get that chutzpah?) Since I'd graduated from high school two years ahead of time and had decided to put off going to Washington University, I'd enrolled at Miss Hickey's, a very well-regarded secretarial school in St. Louis. There were lots of jobs in wartime Washington, Abe insisted, and surely what I had learned at Miss Hickey's would help me get one.

It did. The school helped me find employment at the British Army Liaison Office in Washington, D.C. I moved in with Aunt Fanny and began seeing Abe Pollin every day. He had begun school at the University of Maryland while still working part time for his dad.

But soon Abe was planning again. My parents had a small grocery store in the suburbs of St. Louis, but it was extremely difficult work and required long, arduous travel. Abe suggested that they might like to move to Washington, D.C., and his father and my uncle would help them get started in a business. This was appealing to my parents. They would have a better business opportunity, and live close to family: my aunt, uncle and me. When Abe knew what he wanted, he went after it. But what is extraordinary is the fact that he successfully managed to pull it off. Who takes advice from an eighteen-year-old? Yet, everyone did: his parents, my parents, me.

The next thing I knew, my parents and younger sister, Betty, who was just twelve at the time, moved to Washington. With financial help from Abe's father, they bought a combination grocery and liquor store on the corner of Albemarle and Wisconsin. The four of us moved into the large, cheerful, high-ceilinged apartment above the store. For the first time, Betty and I had a bedroom to ourselves, although we still slept in the same double bed. I loved that old apartment with its high ceilings, tall windows, and a balcony overlooking busy Wisconsin Avenue.

Abe was already enrolled at the University of Maryland, and I left the British Army Staff and joined him there. He lived on the other side of Rock Creek Park. He drove across town every morning to pick me up and then drove back across town again to drive me home when we finished classes. Why did I take this for granted? Our mothers alternated days making lunch sandwiches, which we ate in the dairy. His mother's were fatter than mine. It was 1942 and a strange time to be on a college campus. I joined a sorority, but with a war going on, there were very few boys and little socializing. The campus was both quiet and empty. There was no socializing on campus at all.

I was interested in psychology and took several courses while at Maryland. One course was called "Mental Hygiene"—a strange title for a class that examined various mental disorders, but then people were much less sophisticated about mental illness. Our class took a field trip to St. Elizabeth's, a psychiatric hospital in the District of Columbia that had been the first large-scale, federally run psychiatric hospital in the country. Patients were brought in to talk to our class and answer questions, and psychiatrists lectured us on the symptoms of various mental illnesses. Looking back, the method of introducing these patients was barbaric. Each one was placed in a single chair facing the students. Nonetheless, I was fascinated by the symptoms. If I had realized at the time that some of what I was learning would affect me in a personal way later in my life, and that in fact I would visit St. Elizabeth's again in the future, I would have been less enthralled.

When Abe's father decided to go from plumbing and heating into the construction business, Abe left the University of Maryland to join him. (He ended up graduating from George Washington

University later, after we were married.) Because it was during the war, Abe had no trouble getting building permits, but a lot of trouble getting building materials. As usual, he was extremely resourceful. He would go down to the freight yards at Florida and New York Avenue before dawn and read bills of lading on the boxcars with a flashlight. Then he'd call on a lumber dealer and say, "Sir, you are receiving a shipment of 10,000 board feet of two-by-fours today, and we'd like to buy it." In the business world as in family life, his persistence and thoughtful planning paid off.

The idea of building houses toward the end of the war proved to be brilliant. Suddenly, all the soldiers were coming home and eager to begin families. Hundreds of families lined up to buy the houses as fast as Abe and his father could build them.

This was just the beginning of the post-World War II construction boom. As wartime restrictions on building ended, pent-up housing demand increased, especially since the GI Bill was providing veterans with low-interest rates. Government agencies were also opening new offices in and around Washington, and new highways were encouraging the growth of new residential and commercial communities.

As a result, one of the biggest businesses in Washington had become construction, and the industry was dominated by Eastern European-born Jews who had gone from rags to riches much the way Morris Pollin had. Each one had done it the old fashioned way—by being smart and working hard.

The first of these builders was Morris Cafritz, whose family had immigrated to the United States from Lithuania. He started out owning a grocery store and delivering newspapers in the evenings, and had begun developing residential properties as far back as 1919. By the 1940s, Cafritz was king of construction. His wife, Gwendolyn, had become a celebrated Washington hostess, preferring the company of senators and cabinet officials to builders. By the time Cafritz died in 1964, he had built some 10,000 houses, more than eighty-five apartment buildings and a dozen office buildings.

Morris Pollin was part of the next generation of builders. He considered the Cafritz family to be royalty and gave us vivid descriptions of the annual party he attended at their mansion. Then there were several big builders who followed Abe's father. Charles E. Schmidoff, whose name was changed to Charles E. Smith when he arrived at Ellis Island from Russia, unable to speak English, in the late 1940s, was on his way to developing one of the biggest real estate empires in town. Abraham Kay, who came to the United States as a poor immigrant from Vilna, Russia, began working for $2 a week at a grocery store, eventually owned his own store and then founded Kay Construction Company. Kay also became a prosperous builder of homes and apartment buildings in the Washington, D.C. area. Like Abe's father, all these men actively supported Israel, Jewish causes, as well as many major community institutions: museums, universities, and theaters. They all understood the concept of "giving back."

The other big business in Washington at the time was retail. This business was also dominated by Jewish families, many of which had moved from Baltimore. At the time the biggest stores in the area included the Hecht Company, Kann's Department Store, Hechinger, Lansburgh's, and Garfinckel's—all founded by German Jews, who by and large had been in this country longer than the Russian Jewish builders. Because their ancestors had been in the U.S. longer, they were not comfortable socially with the "newcomers." For a time, there was a distinct separation between the two groups that has since disappeared.

Abe's older brother Jack was in the military, fortunately stationed in London. Abe's mother wanted us to wait to get married until he returned, but by this time we had been dating for three years and we felt we had waited long enough. In May 1945 (just three months before his brother came home, as it turned out) we were married at

Washington, D.C.'s Hamilton Hotel. (Actor/dancer Gene Kelly was staying at the hotel that weekend, and the guests were thrilled to keep seeing him in his uniform in the elevator.) We honeymooned in New York City, but this time turned out to be quite different from my first visit. We stayed at the beautiful St. Moritz (in a quite small room) and ate breakfast at the wonderful Rumpelmayer's restaurant on the first floor of the hotel. For me, it was all a beautiful dream. We tried to get into some fancy nightclubs, but Abe didn't understand that he needed to tip the headwaiter to get a table. We were very young and unsophisticated.

So much of the talking that we did during the three years we had been dating was about the future, about having a family. We both wanted to have lots of children. We were naïve, and innocent. But we knew the life we wanted to have and we talked endlessly about that life. Abe was one of three and I was one of two. We both wanted to create a bigger family than those we grew up in.

When I became pregnant in 1946, we were thrilled. I wanted so much to do everything right. I chose a doctor, Bernard Notes, who delivered without anesthetics in a more natural way. One of his ideas was not to gain too much weight, so I was extremely careful and only gained 10 pounds. I did everything right, including having my bag packed for the hospital well in advance. I was ready to go walk out of the door when the critical moment arrived.

I began having labor pains on the night of Saturday, April 5 and within five minutes I had picked up my suitcase and was on my way out the door, only to discover my husband carefully examining the ties in his closet, trying to decide which one he would wear.

"What is taking you so long?" I asked with my hand on the doorknob.

"I'm putting on a suit and tie," he calmly said. "Tomorrow is Easter Sunday."

Our daughter, Linda Joy Pollin, was born early in the morning on April 6, 1947, Easter Sunday. We named her "Linda" after a song that was popular at that time and "Joy" because she was our first child, a joy to us. She was beautiful and looked just like her father with her turned-up nose and curly blond hair. I was so pleased that she looked like him. I always wanted a turned-up nose. Later that day when I awoke from a nap in my hospital room, I couldn't believe what my eyes were seeing: birds flying around the room. As I focused, the "birds" turned out to be the birds-of-paradise—flowers that Abe had sent. I had never seen those flowers before. Lying in my hospital bed with my beautiful daughter in my arms, looking at the exotic flowers my husband had sent me, was a moment of joy in my life never to be repeated.

Abe and I couldn't have been happier. My parents were delighted too. This was their first grandchild. We all looked Linda Joy over carefully and agreed that she was perfect. Even her little shape was perfect. What we couldn't check out was what we couldn't see, and that turned out to be her heart. Her heart was not perfect. It was several months before our pediatrician told us that she had a congenital heart condition.

Actually, until she began crawling and taking first steps, her condition wasn't noticeable. But when she began walking and later, running, her lips would turn blue and she would get out of breath. The condition was sometimes referred to as a "blue baby." The scientific term for her condition was "Tetralogy of Fallot." Heart abnormalities inhibit the flow of blood to the lungs and prevent the blood from getting as much oxygen as it needs.

As she was growing and increasingly more active, I began watching her very closely. Whenever I saw her lips turning blue, I would pick her up. I didn't want her to get tired. I would swoop her up, put her in the stroller, or carry her in my arms. This became second nature to me. When I took her to the local park with other mothers and children, I always picked her up the minute I noticed her change in color. I didn't want the other mothers to notice that she had a problem. I didn't want anyone to know about her condition.

This was not my idea. My mother-in-law told us not to tell anyone, even my own mother and sister. I don't know whether she thought if we didn't mention it, the problem would go away or if she was ashamed to have a less-than-perfect grandchild. But we were young and totally inexperienced in dealing with something like this, and we dutifully—stupidly—followed his mother's wishes; Abe more willingly than I. (I found out later that she had been telling her side of the family about Linda's problems all along, and telling them that the cause of the heart condition came from my side of the family.)

After a while, I found I could not keep this up. It was completely against my nature to hide something, especially something that I wasn't ashamed of. How could I keep something like this from my own mother?

I finally told my parents, but we told no one else. None of our friends knew for years.

I hadn't told my sister either. But when Linda was one-and-a-half, Betty and I went to Atlantic City with her for a week. But even before we left, I knew that at some point I would have to tell her. I couldn't hide it forever.

We had a terrific time playing with Linda, who was a happy, adorable child. But every morning I woke up terrified that this might be the day I would have to tell my sister. Finally one day I just blurted it out. Betty was shocked—not so much at the heart problem, as at the fact that I had waited so long to tell her. I hadn't realized how tense holding in this secret had made me, and how relieved I was to be able to open up to my sister. What a mistake that was to keep this terrible information from the people I was closest to.

That time together in Atlantic City was a special, bonding experience. Betty was six years younger than I, which was a big age gap when we were growing up. I always considered her my "darling baby sister," but now that we were twenty-four and eighteen, that gap shrunk. I was proud of her. She was tall, even a little taller than me, and had beautiful rich, dark curly brown hair. She also had a beautiful singing voice and had had voice lessons, hoping to have a career in music. She also was a natural performer, something I never was. I didn't even envy that. I was just too plain shy and scared.

Family ties had always been very important to both of us growing up, and her love for my daughter gave us a new kind of family pleasure to share. Back in Washington, she soon began to babysit for us in our apartment.

When Linda was three-and-a-half, I took her to Florida for the winter for the second time. The doctor advised us to do this so she wouldn't have to deal with the cold weather in Washington. It was lonely without Abe, but this is what we had to do.

As we were walking home from the beach one early afternoon, I spotted an orange juice stand with an awning. Deciding it would be good to get her out of the heat, I stopped and sat her on the counter. As I did this, the man behind the counter smiled at us and said "What a cute little girl!" Then he said, "She seems to be cold. Her lips are blue."

I had lied so many times before, but I decided this might be an opportunity for me to test how he would react if I told him the truth. I did not know him and I probably would never see him again. With my heart pounding for what seemed like forever, I looked at Linda and thought, *This is my chance to tell someone, someone I don't have to worry about because he's a stranger.*

"No, she isn't cold," I mumbled. "She has a heart condition." And then I waited anxiously to hear his response.

"Oh, I'm sorry," he said.

That was it! A simple statement had yielded a simple, drama-free response. I had at last broken my vow of silence. I felt a huge sense of relief. The world hadn't come crashing down. I could be free to explain her condition. I no longer had to hide it. Her condition was nothing to be ashamed of. The pain in my chest went away. Now, I had the option to discuss her condition or not as I chose. And I didn't always want to discuss it either; it depended on who asked or under what circumstances. As time went by, I never wanted anyone to feel sorry either for Linda or me. But, I no longer had to keep this information buried inside.

I took her down from the fruit-stand counter and my refreshed daughter and I walked home.

Our pediatrician recommended we have Linda monitored regularly, and we did. Every year we took her for a checkup and a heart catheterization or coronary angiogram at Johns Hopkins Hospital in Baltimore. There she was cared for by two of the most famous heart specialists at the time—surgeon, Dr. Alfred Blalock and cardiologist Dr. Helen Taussig—the team who had developed the first successful "blue baby" operation. Over the years, we grew very close to Dr. Taussig. We looked up to her as our god. Our child's life was in her hands, as well as was ours.

When Linda was four years old, Dr. Taussig told us that she needed bypass surgery. In 1951 it was still a new and dangerous procedure, but we didn't have a choice; the only choice was when. In fact, the procedure was still so new that there was only one nurse in all of Baltimore who could take care of her post-op. Fortunately, they were able to find Goldie Hutchison. Linda did well with the surgery.

After a few weeks we were able to bring her home, where I took care of her. Her lips were now pink instead of blue, and she still woke every morning with a smile on her face. But for me, I had to look at my darling little four-year-old's body with a huge scar across her small chest. She also had a deep abscess on her arm from so many shots, which also left a deep scar. But the positive result was all that mattered. This was one of the first heart bypass surgeries and it had worked, enabling more oxygen to flow to her heart. She would now be able to function almost normally for a number of years. Sometime in the future—twelve years from then—she would need more surgery. That was something we could live with. Right now our daughter could have a normal life. The future was far away.

Age sixteen seems a century away when your child is four.

In 1950 I became pregnant with Robert. We were eager to go on to have the big family we wanted, fully expecting any other children we had would be normal and healthy. The chances of having a child with heart problems were quite rare, and the chances of having it happen twice were even rarer. And this time, we were lucky. Robert turned out to be a big, strong, beautiful, happy, healthy baby. Like our daughter, he had blond curly hair, big blue eyes, and also woke each morning with a smile. He was just a much bigger version. We were thrilled to have our family grow, and my husband now had a son with whom he could share his love of sports. I had to learn to cope with a boy; no boys in my family. What a joyful time in our lives!

I became pregnant again in 1952, and we were thrilled. This time it was another boy—once again big with blond curly hair and sapphire-blue eyes. We named him Kenneth Jay and decided to call him "Jay Jay" for short. The pediatrician not only declared him strong and healthy but added, "This one is going to be a football player!" Abe and I were thrilled. Our family was beginning to look like our dreams. And, my athletic husband was thrilled to have two big strong boys!

Unfortunately, Dr. Weinstein completely missed the diagnosis. Within a few weeks, I began to notice that Jay Jay was having trouble sucking his bottle. Then, one Sunday afternoon while my in-laws were visiting and as I was changing Jay Jay on his bathinette, he passed out. As I stood over him in shock and panic, my mother-in-law just happened to walk by the door to his room. As she came into the room, seeing me in a state of terror, she said, "Don't tell Abe!"

"Don't tell Abe?" I cried, running to find him. "Don't tell Abe?" My baby was so sick and she's telling me not to tell my husband? That was the last time I ever listened to what she said to me. I matured many years in those few moments.

Soon Jay Jay could barely take food before he passed out. His diagnosis was similar to Linda's, but his condition was so much worse.

By the time he was six months old, he was listless and could barely eat or drink. Trying to feed him became almost impossible, and then he began to swell.

"You have to take him to Baltimore immediately," my pediatrician said when I finally called and described his condition. "He's in heart failure."

How well I remember that ride on that hot summer day. There were no cellphones in those days. I couldn't reach Abe at work, and having no alternative, I put Jay Jay in the car and drove him to Johns Hopkins myself.

The entire ride I was alternately veering through the traffic on the main road to Baltimore and checking him in the car seat, praying that we would make it to the hospital in time for him to get emergency care (before he died in the car).

That was a time when hospitals had strict rules and regulations about feeding and everything else. Here I was alone with my desperately ill infant who had tremendous difficulty swallowing because his breathing was so labored, and he needed to be fed gradually, any time he could manage it. Yet, hospital rules and intransigence wouldn't allow me to keep his bottle in his room. I begged and pleaded with the nurses to let me just keep one bottle in the small sink by his bed, but they refused. It was against the rules. They were the ones who controlled who could have the bottles and when. And when I couldn't leave the room for fear he'd pass out, I would ring for any nurse, and wait and wait. When she arrived, I'd tell her I needed a bottle. She would then go back to get a bottle, and again I would wait and wait. All this time, Jay Jay was crying, then screaming, then turning blue. By the time the nurse finally brought me the bottle, he had often become too weak to take it. I was terrified and angry and alone.

By the second day, I became so upset and frustrated with the conditions in the hospital that I just picked up Jay Jay and walked out of the hospital, into the street and ran with him in my arms down the dirty streets of old Baltimore, not knowing where I was or where I was headed. I wasn't even thinking clearly enough to be frightened. All I wanted to do was to get away from the hospital and the nurses who would not listen to me. After running for several blocks in the hot summer heat, and thinking about what I would do next, I realized that I had not taken my handbag. I had no way to get home. Had I remembered, Jay Jay and I would have been in a cab, heading for Washington. But I had no handbag and therefore no money. I had no choice but to walk back to the hospital. The nurses had not even missed me.

There was no doubt that Jay Jay needed emergency surgery. At the time there were no surgeons at Johns Hopkins who could operate on a six-month-old infant. The only option was to bring in a specialist from Chicago, but could we bring him in fast enough? The surgeon agreed to fly overnight and operate the next day.

Miraculously, Jay Jay managed to come through the surgery, but he never thrived after that. That summer we went to Atlantic City with Linda and Robert. Jay Jay seemed better, but by the fall he was once again doing poorly. At home we had oxygen tents over his crib and, at one point, I had to have a nurse help me care for him.

Eventually, there was no choice but to go back to Johns Hopkins. I stayed there with him for three months, sleeping on a cot in his room as he went in and out of oxygen tents. The doctors told Abe and I there was nothing more they could do. In a total state of denial, I truly believed that if I could just take him home, I could cure him.

But that New Year's Eve, the doctors told us he wasn't going to make it and suggested we go home and spend a little time with our two young children. We did come home for that one night, and then spent the next month-and-a-half watching him slowly weaken. One night in February, I decided to come home for a night. I received a call from one of the nurses the next morning. Jay Jay had died. A nurse had taken him for a stroll in the hall, and he developed pneumonia. I was very angry with her for doing that, but later realized it was inevitable.

I've often worried that Jay Jay's illness and death was a tough time for both my children, but particularly for Robert. He was just two years old, and I was away a lot in the hospital—once for three months. When I was home, I was totally preoccupied with a very sick baby lying helpless in his crib. Often between checking on the oxygen tent, I would look into the living room where I could see Robert was playing happily. I well remember my feelings of relief when I saw him contented and happy.

I was grateful for his easygoing nature and good health, but concerned that because he was so robust—and had two siblings who required more care—he wasn't getting his fair share of attention. There wasn't much that I could do about the situation. That was what we had to deal with.

Jay Jay's death was a turning point for Abe and me. We had worried as two of our children had managed to come through life-threatening surgeries. We had spent four years preoccupied with caring for sick children. We had gone from the youthful optimism of being sure that nothing bad could happen to the unbearable pain of losing a beautiful little boy.

There are times in your life when you just keep going, and Jay Jay's death was one of them. It was a gut-wrenching experience, made more agonizing for me because Abe and I never discussed it. Often, at night, when we were alone in our bedroom, I would ask, "Why aren't we talking about him?"

But Abe simply could not talk about Jay Jay's death. In his family, you didn't talk about feelings, especially painful ones; you kept things inside. You tried to bury them, get rid of them that way.

I lived with a pain in my chest for a long time.

Gradually, the children helped pull us out of it. We still had two beautiful children and we became happily busy with them. Linda was seven by this time, going to school, and Robert was three. Linda was doing very well after her surgery. Her life was quite normal. She wrote poetry and had a column in the school newspaper that she shared with a girlfriend. As always, our children were the most important things in our lives.

Not surprising for siblings, Robert and Linda had very different personalities. Robert was always a big, happy youngster and very sports oriented, while Linda was an avid reader and writer. At the dinner table neither one really dominated. Abe and I thoroughly enjoyed our meals with them. We'd hear about their school activities, who said what to whom, and we'd hear about what sports figure Robert was emulating at the moment. Abe was delighted to have a sports buddy. Family dinners were sacrosanct in the sense that Abe never missed one. Despite being a very busy man, he was home every night at six or six thirty, and always called to let me know he was on his way. Our children and our family occupied our lives.

Socially, we saw a lot of the second-generation Washington builders —the sons and daughters of the men of Morris Pollin's generation—either at the Woodmont Country Club or at Jewish fundraisers. My father-in-law bought us tickets to just about every Jewish fundraiser there was—UJA, Israeli Bonds, you name it— as did their fathers. We all obediently attended, usually in formal attire, to support the cause.

Abe's family and mine were similar in many respects, but different in others. Both were Jewish and shared similar values. My father-in-law had made a lot of money, and while he was very generous with his whole family, his relationship with his wife was not good. It was not unusual to have Abe's parents start screaming at each other in the middle of family get-togethers. My parents, on the other hand, had always worked together as partners in business, and were very loving and respectful toward one another. They shared their work, as well as all family decisions. I remember often hearing my parents talking quietly late into the night about how they would deal with the problems they faced, business, their future.

This was a completely different household from Abe's. While Abe's home was chaotic, mine was secure. And even though Abe's family had dinner together and my parents were working, the atmosphere was at completely opposite ends. I craved company and Abe craved peace.

Abe and I replicated my parents' relationship. We were always partners. In the beginning I'm sure this was more my doing than his, but it intensified as the years went on. He brought home the building plans and I designed the interiors. This not only brought us closer, it also brought me closer to my father-in-law. He was the first person I ever knew who wanted to take everything he could out of life.

We went to the Pollin house for dinner every Friday night and to my family's every Sunday night. When we were with my in-laws, I loved listening to the way my father-in-law planned his days, always conscious of including something pleasurable for himself, such as music lessons or exercise. Morris Pollin was a man with a real zest for life. He and I shared a love of travel.

When my father-in-law was in his late forties, he announced, "I'm going to retire." This was a man who was in excellent health and had been successful in business and simply decided it was time to enjoy his life. He had been working since he was nine years old as a plumber.

He not only spoke of what he planned to do; he did it. Against his wife's wishes, they took a trip around the world. And when he was in Washington, he became involved in the local community giving generously to schools, synagogues, and community centers.

He had dreamed of taking violin lessons his entire life, and unfortunately, he did that too. He had a terrible ear for music, but we all overlooked that. He loved playing the violin and so be it.

I especially respected his sense of proportion—the importance of balance in his life. He carefully measured every hour in his day to accomplish what he wanted.

One day he announced to his two eldest sons, Jack and Abe, "I'm going to Florida for the whole winter. This is your business now. You're on your own."

Abe was terrified, but ready. He had been working in the office and on the construction jobs for years. His older brother Jack preferred having a good time to working, and Abe ended up doing all the work. It was not a fair arrangement.

One day in 1957, I confronted Abe on this mismatch. "Why don't we go out on our own?" I suggested. "You're carrying the whole business anyway."

We sat for many days and hours on our bed, going over the pros and cons. Finally, bucking enormous pressure to stay with the family business, Abe made the decision to begin building apartment houses on our own. He was extremely reluctant to break away from the family business, which he had been part of for so long. But he knew it was something he had to do, to be his own man.

We did all of the building planning together. He'd bring home the floor plans and I'd look at them to see if there were better ways to use the space—move this closet over there and move the bathroom over here. I designed the lobbies and did the interior spaces. I loved doing it. We worked together extremely well. He put up the buildings and I did the interiors. It was an exciting and satisfying time for both of us.

After we lost Jay Jay, we wanted to have more children. We still wanted the large family. I'd had easy pregnancies and was willing to try again, but Dr. Taussig said that even though it was extremely rare to have two children with severe heart problems she didn't think we should try it again. We were bereft, but had one option: to adopt.

We decided to adopt not realizing how long that process could take, particularly because of the path we decided to take. And it did take a long time—five years to be exact—but we waited.

One day, the Jewish Social Service Agency in Washington called us with good news. They wanted us to come and see the baby boy they felt was right for us. And, seeing him in his bassinette, bright eyed and smiling, it was an immediate "yes."

Jimmy was just a few months old when we adopted him. He was a little dynamo, and the kids were delighted. When we brought him home, Linda was in her room with a cold. She insisted that she have a peek so we opened the door a tiny bit so she could see, but not infect him.

Robert, on the other hand, went running out on the street, knocking on all the neighbors' doors, announcing: "I have a brother! I have a new brother!" Both children were very excited to have a baby brother. As she did so often, Linda expressed her feelings in poetry.

> *My little brother Jim,*
> *Not very neat or prim*
> *But very cute and tough*
> *And very, very rough*
> *He makes me very gay*
> *And always wants to play*
> *He's eleven months old*
> *Simply made of gold*
> *My brother Jim*

From the moment we brought him home, Jimmy was high energy, very high energy, always. At night, when he was ten months old, we'd put him in his crib upstairs thinking he was asleep, but then we would suddenly find him sitting at the head of the stairs. If I took him shopping with me, he would be crawling under all the dress racks. As a result, I received very good service. They couldn't wait to get me out of the store. He began walking when he was ten months old. He loved crawling into Linda's bed in the morning. In a letter from camp when Jimmy was two, Linda wrote about a movie she had seen the night before:

> At the end of the movie was a baby. He looked exactly like Jimmy. It made me feel so homesick. Do you think he'll recognize me when I come home? I sure hope so.

We were a very happy family.

Abe liked the idea of naming all his buildings after our family members. The first one was an attractive light brick building at 14th and Military Road that he named "The Lynwood" after Linda. That was the first building that I helped design. "Robert Towers" named after Robert was the first building we built on our own. After that, the buildings we built grew in scale. There was the James (after Jimmy) and later, when we had used up the children's names, there was "The Rittenhouse" on 16th Street and "The Crestwood." Jimmy and Robert loved going to the construction jobs and getting tractor rides. Linda, who loved to write on the typewriter, came up with fake advertisements. "Come all you young married couples," one urged. "Find romance by moving into the Rittenhouse!"

Then came the Apolliné. That unusual name came from a wonderful dinner we had with Joe Abel, the architect, and his wife, Marge. After working together on so many buildings, we had become quite good friends. We were feeling very relaxed after delicious food and several glasses of wine, and we began playing with various names for the next building. There hadn't been a building named after me, but I felt the name "Irene" was not euphonic enough. We decided it was time to name one after my husband. There were lots of laughs and crazy combinations, but when Marge came up with the idea of blending Abe's first initial,

"A" with his last name and making it sound French and exclusive, we went for it. Apolliné with an accent aigu on the e! *Nobody* would be able to pronounce it, but that would be part of the fun.

These were good times. We had three delightful children who kept us on our toes and a wonderful social life, particularly within Washington's Jewish community—the people we saw most frequently at the various fundraisers my father-in-law still bought us tickets to attend.

=============

My sister Betty's beautiful singing voice earned her a place at the Washington Opera Society. She was very young—just a little over 20—when she got married. Her first child was a darling, lively girl: Ilene. When she went into labor with her second child, Howard, I stayed with her during her entire labor. It was a strange time because she couldn't stop talking about a close friend she had who had just suffered a nervous breakdown and had been placed in St. Elizabeth's, the public mental hospital I'd visited as a student at Maryland.

"It's happening to me too, Irene," she confided in me, "I feel as though I have what she has."

"Don't be silly, Betty," I assured her. "You're just wrought up because you know her and you're about to have a baby!"

"I'm going to end up in St. Elizabeth's," Betty cried.

I tried to reassure her that she was fine and not like her friend.

This was the 1950s. Mental illness was something people whispered about. There was no doubt she was terrified, even as I tried to reassure her. She gave birth to her second child, Howard—a beautiful boy—and in the excitement surrounding the arrival of this newest member of the family, we forgot about her worries.

But they lingered. It turned out Betty was not all right. She was hearing voices, behaving strangely. As her erratic behavior became more and more apparent, her husband, Jack, and my parents arranged for her to go to Sheppard Pratt, a well-regarded mental hospital in Baltimore.

She spent a month there and, when she came home, she seemed much better, calmer than I had seen her in a while. Jack was working for my parents in their liquor store as he had from the time they were married.

Thinking that perhaps they needed some privacy and a fresh start, Abe and I encouraged the two of them to go out on their own, maybe even look for something outside of Washington, hoping change would help Betty's mental condition.

They didn't take our suggestion, but it probably would not have helped even if they had. The signs of a more severe mental illness were becoming more noticeable. This was my baby sister. I adored her, and I had no idea what to do.

She began behaving even more strangely and erratically. She would decide suddenly, for example, that she had to get out of the house, putting her two young children in a car and driving around the city; we knew not where. As time passed, the voices she had been hearing became more constant, more pronounced, gradually giving rise to violent outbreaks.

My mother and I were beginning to fear not only for her own safety, but for the safety of her children as well. This time the doctors recommended a stay at Chestnut Lodge, a private psychiatric clinic near Washington. My mother and I visited her regularly, hoping for some sort of cure, but it never seemed to happen. Little did we know at the time that she would spend the next ten years of her life there. Chestnut Lodge was a beautiful facility, but her treatment wasn't working. She had to be more and more heavily medicated. She never recovered.

One day I was visiting Betty in her room on the second floor at Chestnut Lodge when, for no discernable reason, she became furious and tried to attack me. I was terrified. I was, I thought, at least as strong as my sister physically, but I knew that I was up against something stronger than myself. I went running out of her room and down the nearby stairs as fast as I could. I was extremely frightened for myself, and terrified for Betty, too.

What was happening to my sister?

=============

I wanted so much for Linda to have as normal a life as possible. That was my goal from the day we learned of her diagnosis—for her to do as much as she could and not feel afraid or handicapped. That goal established my modus operandi in raising her; it became my unspoken raison d'etre.

Making everything flow normally took constant thought, planning, and attentiveness. I was always alert. In 1960, we decided to build the house we had been planning for ten years. I looked all over the city and saw some beautiful properties overlooking Rock Creek Park, but any place where there were lots of steps or an uphill climb was out of the question. It had to be a place where she could function without worrying about getting tired; where she could live her life with as little concern as possible about normal daily activities.

When considering schools, camps, and outings with friends, I constantly made calculations as to how much energy would be required, but always behind the scenes. I never wanted her to know of my planning.

When she was young, I knew what her limitations were and watched carefully to make sure she didn't exceed them. How many steps would she have to climb at school? How hard would it be for her to walk that distance with her classmates? I don't think I realized back then how much this thinking preoccupied me, and I'm sure Linda didn't either. It became second nature. As she got older, she knew what she could and couldn't do, but I don't think she ever felt restricted. She knew her limitations and accepted them.

I did not want to hover over her. Her health became a fact of life rather than a handicap. We never really talked about it, but she knew her limitations because she would get tired. True, there were things she couldn't do, but there was so much that she could do—that she did do. We always emphasized the positive. I wanted her to feel free, and I think it worked. Her view of herself reflected that. She was a happy and positive child, a self-confident little girl, an upbeat, outgoing teenager. In the mornings, when I went to wake her up for school, she went almost instantaneously from eyes closed to a smile. She greeted each day that way. My nickname for her was "Lindy Lou."

When we sent her to camp, I arranged for the counselor to keep an eye out for her, and she did. Linda went away to camp for many summers and loved them all. *"Please send stationery, jacks, a pink Spalding hi bounce ball and cookies,"* she wrote in one letter after explaining that she dressed as "Switzerland" in a camp United Nations contest by wearing a yellow cloth with holes in it. (*"Swiss cheese, get it?"*)

She had a wonderful sense of humor and loved to write. *"Dear Legal Parents,"* a note we found when we came home from a party one night began. *Tonight at around 8:45 a policeman named Officer A McNeil came and asked if we had a collie dog. He said this morning around 10:00 a maid (address on another page) was very mildly bitten by a collie and it probably is our Lady. He also asked us questions, which Robert and I answered. For 14 days you need to keep Lady indoors, and call up the police if she gets sick or is killed. Then you can let her out, he explained.*

> *As soon as you get home, Robert wants*
> *you to wake him up.*
> *So do I.*
> *Love Linda*
> *P.S. It might have been the dog around*
> *Woodland Drive, whose name is Skippy*
> *(I think).*

As she got older, her writing reflected her warmth and became more profound. An anniversary card to us begins:

You have made me what I am, and so far I have never been
ashamed of myself.
You have taught me of life, and so far I have never
felt ignorant.
You have given me love, and so far I have never
felt loneliness.
You have taught me religion, and so far I can win any
argument about God.
You have helped me to try and follow your footsteps along
the road of life, and so far I hope my feet are headed in
the right direction.
Have the most happy anniversary in the whole history of time!
Your sincerely loving daughter, Linda

By the time Linda Joy was 14, however, her condition began to change. Whenever she became ill with flu or a bad cold, she had a harder time shaking it off than other children. We were beginning to see the future that the doctors had predicted. She was now fully grown and developed, and her body needed the necessary oxygen. Always in the back of our minds we had known this stage was coming, but now it was upon us. Her sixteenth year was fast approaching and so was the operation that was necessary for her to have a normal life.

When she was four years old she had heart bypass surgery, but this surgical procedure was more serious; it meant penetrating the heart. It required going inside the heart to make the necessary corrections. It was what she needed to survive "healthily ever after." We had been looking forward to this moment for twelve years. This procedure would enable her to go to college, get married, and have the children she so badly wanted.

Even though we all knew what was in the future for her, we never discussed it except as a given. And even though Linda and

I were always very close—we had long talks at bedtime every night, either on her bed or mine—I can only remember one time she asked me details about her illness. A few weeks before her upcoming Sweet Sixteen birthday party, which was a month before her surgery, sitting in the car on our way to a party store, she asked, "Do I have the same thing that Jay Jay had?" Taken aback, I said no. I struggled with my answer. I had always been honest with her; I couldn't be anything else now. The "no" answer was technically correct. They had a similar condition, but his was much worse. I was telling most of the truth.

We talked many times about the surgery, but always the positive side. This is something that she wanted; something we all wanted. She knew that to be able to lead a normal life as an adult, she would need to be stronger, healthier. There was only one alternative—the surgery. The only question was when, and the timing seemed to be now, while she was still strong enough to undergo this dangerous procedure.

We felt as confident as we could be. The surgery would be done at Johns Hopkins by Dr. David Sabiston, the cardiac surgeon she had known almost her entire life.

I was prepared in my own way. I fully expected that she would have as excellent a result as she'd had when she was four. I never considered any other possibility. Afterward, she could lead a strong, normal life.

Of course, we were all worried. Any time you're having heart surgery, you're worried. They told us there were dangers with this surgery, but Linda was so alive—a graceful, beautiful, ostensibly healthy teenager who had just celebrated her birthday with a wonderful party filled with friends. She had even traveled to Austria with a travel camp a month earlier. We fully expected she was going to come out fine, better than fine. This would give her the life she had wanted for so long, the life we wanted for her for so long.

I think the waiting room where we awaited the results was darkish and nondescript. But, to be truthful, it might have been colorful with pictures on the wall. Waiting rooms are just that—rooms where you wait for a verdict, rooms where your preoccupation with that verdict tends to render the immediate surroundings invisible. My mind and thoughts stood still. Time stood still.

Abe and I held hands as we waited. We always held hands. When he had asked for permission to do so as a shy seventeen-year-old boy, Abe had unknowingly ushered in a lifetime of hand holding. I still remember the comforting feel of his fingers in mine. Feeling Abe's closeness, I reviewed the positives. We had known her surgeon for sixteen years, ever since Linda's birth, when he had been just a resident, and we would bring her to Hopkins for yearly exams and consultations. We had complete faith in him. We knew he would bring her to a new state of health.

And we had faith in Linda, who had cheerfully brought her guitar with her to the hospital so she could practice, along with the names and addresses of all her friends, so she could write to them as she convalesced. Linda had come through heart surgery before with flying colors, and she would do so again. This surgery was going to give her an extra boost—a bridge to the future. We had all been looking forward to this moment for twelve years.

I'm not sure when it hit me. When I saw the way the doctor approached us? When I caught the expression in his eyes? This was more than our surgeon, after all; this was a man with whom we had personal ties—a sixteen-year relationship. Whatever the signal was that I got, my eyes were peeled to the expression on his face.

"We hit a nerve," Dr. Sabiston said, not looking at us directly, and so softly I could barely hear him. Four words. I'm sure he said more, but that was all I remember. That meant that her heart could no longer function; Linda could no longer function. Four words and all the hoping was over. Linda was over. A crucial, precious part of our lives was over.

Linda lived for two weeks after we learned the results, on and off a ventilator. Those were extremely difficult weeks for all three of us. We didn't have to tell her what was happening, she knew. She grew weaker and weaker. I remember holding her hand and every day combing her beautiful blond curly hair.

The night before she died, she was in the intensive care unit and her kidneys were going. All Abe and I could do was to just stand there next to the bed, holding her hand. She was unaware that we were there. But as we stood watching her sleep, I heard a loud clicking sound. I looked around the bed to see where it was coming from and I saw a bright halo surrounding her head. Could I actually be seeing this? Was I hallucinating? Maybe I was, but it was as clear to me then as it is now as I write it.

I didn't tell Abe; I didn't tell anyone. I was still holding her hand, when the nurse said we should leave. Reluctant to pull my hand away from hers, the nurse put a piece of smooth wood in Linda's hand in place of my hand. It was extremely painful for me to leave her bed, and I still remember looking back with the nurse standing over her.

As we left the intensive care unit and began walking down the large, dark, high-ceilinged hallways, I wanted to scream. Holding onto each other's hands as tightly as we could, Abe and I walked toward the light pouring through the tall entrance ahead of us. During this walk, which I thought would never end, I held in the scream building inside of me; a scream of such intensity that I thought if I released it, it would destroy the world. Oh, how I wanted to scream, loud enough for the entire world to hear. "I lost my daughter!" But I didn't scream.

I remember the many stone steps—almost two stories high—that led down to the street outside the John Hopkins Medical Center. Holding on to each other as tightly as we could, Abe and I made our way down those broad white stone steps…all those steps. I thought they would never end.

That was June 1963. When we got home and I went to her room, I found a notebook with her attempts to complete a poem about her feelings.

> The sun beats upon my back,
> My body dry,
> Water, water.
> But none – sand, heat, hell
> My body bends
> My lips quiver
> God, water!
> My camel stops,
> He kneels.
> My help cometh from the Lord.
> Water in the distance
> Closer, closer.
> The water disappeared.
> The land is dry,
> My help cometh from the Lord.
> My heart slows down.
> Thump… thump…
> Silence prevails
> My thirst is quenched.

I was completely surprised. With all of the nightly long talks and thoughts shared over the years, she never expressed any thoughts about dying. I had never realized the depth of her thinking. What an incredible poem! It was beautiful, but not frightening. There were many rough drafts. Obviously, she had struggled for a long time. In page after page, she never displayed any fear; only an acceptance that I did not have and did not know that she had. She was prepared for any eventuality. I was not. I had no idea of the kind of maturity she had reached.

Linda's death was devastating for Abe and me, but it also proved devastating for the whole family. Robert and Jimmy had seen their sister prior to the surgery, when she seemed just as she'd always seemed—perfectly healthy—and they never saw her again. Robert did not want to talk about it. Five-year-old Jimmy, who adored his big sister and loved to climb into her bed to snuggle, didn't know what to make of it. Where was Linda?

"But, but, where *is* she?"

Grandparents normally don't bury grandchildren. Linda's death was a devastating shock to my parents.

Little did I know as we mourned Linda that her death was just the beginning of what would turn out to be "The Year from Hell" for the entire family.

Robert's bar mitzvah had been scheduled for that September. We knew he would do an incredible job, because Robert was a natural. He was a tall, handsome teenager, and a natural speaker, but unfortunately he didn't get a chance to show off his talents to friends and family. My father died suddenly of a heart attack the day before the bar mitzvah was supposed to occur. The bar mitzvah as planned never happened. According to Jewish tradition, we had a ceremony in the synagogue with the immediate family and no celebration.

I have no memory of my father's funeral and remember little of Robert's bar mitzvah. By that time I was on some very powerful medications to help me cope with my grief. Then my sister, whose mental health had been declining for years, was diagnosed as having paranoid schizophrenia. Throughout all this, it was my mother who managed to hold everything together. My father, the love of her life, had died suddenly. They had been inseparable throughout their married life, working together, planning together. But when he died, she had no time to mourn. She was too busy taking care of me, who had become a basket case over the loss of my daughter. She was also taking care of Ilene and Howard, the two young children my sister had left behind when she was institutionalized.

Nothing seemed to stop my mother from doing whatever it took to hold what was left of the family together. She was amazingly strong.

Too strong, it turned out. While caring for Betty's children, just eight months after my father's death, my mother had a heart attack and died two weeks later. Prior to this entire crisis, she had been quite healthy and energetic with no sign of any heart problem. She was sixty-three and didn't have a wrinkle on her face. But so much tragedy had happened so fast. She had lost her granddaughter, lost her daughter to mental illness, and lost her lifetime partner—all in a matter of months. I think her heart could only take so much.

I felt like a Holocaust victim. I had just lost my mother, father, sister, and daughter in a little over a year.

"I'm your family now," Abe told me, and he was my family. How many nights did we sit together just holding hands, experiencing an unbearable sense of loss? Why did our daughter have to die? Why did we lose a son? To have two children with this very rare genetic disease—two children!

I was a zombie, taking as much Valium and Librium as it took to dull all feeling. One day ran into the next. Friends did what they thought they should do, but I simply wasn't up to going to lunch and pretending all was okay. My life had changed; I had changed. I was not the person I used to be. I couldn't meet friends in the mental place I used to meet them—a place we had shared—and very few were comfortable about meeting me where I was. Fortunately, there were some exceptions—two close friends who understood where I was at. I needed to talk and they listened.

I sought psychiatric help, but psychiatry at the time didn't deal well with grief or mourning. I didn't need to go back to my childhood to examine the personal interactions of my early years; I needed help in my mourning. I was not a depressed person. The misery I was experiencing was completely normal given the circumstances. I tried a number of therapists, but none worked.

Thanks to the drugs they put me on, I basically spent the next year in a fog.

It was a year of treading water, a year of just barely functioning. My children Robert and Jimmy were there, but I wasn't there for them.

How did my husband handle his grief? Abe tried to go to work, but decided he wanted to build a loving memorial for Linda, something to do with children, young people. First, we created a scholarship for a young woman in Israel. Then we created an apartment complex, the Linda Pollin Memorial Housing Project, a nonprofit in Southeast Washington for people with children. Again, we sat on our bed with the plans spread out. We wanted to build large apartments to accommodate families, with a recreation building and a pool. In later years, we would run into people who told us how their lives were changed as a result of growing up there.

There are defining moments in everyone's life—moments when incredible, powerful changes occur. Often they come about from something one dreams about. But ours came about not from something we wanted, but from the worst nightmare possible; not from something we did, but from something that happened to us. We were both in terrible pain and searching for a way to move forward with our lives. We were still in our late thirties. Our whole lives were ahead of us. What could we do?

One evening in 1964, Abe told me about a phone call he received that day. "A guy called me today and asked me if I was interested in buying a piece of the Baltimore Bullets basketball team.

What do you think?"

I didn't answer right away but my thinking was "no." I needed him badly. This would take him away.

"This would be good for both of us," he told me. "You love sports. You are always saying how you loved going to baseball games in St. Louis."

"That was baseball, and I was a kid," I told him.

"This could take us away from our sadness, Irene. This could be just the kind of distraction we need."

The more I thought about it, the more I thought Abe might be right. This idea was just crazy enough, just unusual and consuming enough to pull us both out of the funk we had been living in for so long.

Jimmy was seven and had no idea of what lay ahead, but our in-house avid sports enthusiast, fourteen-year-old Robert, needed no convincing. "Do it Dad!" Robert urged. "You're gonna become famous!"

So that year, Abe and I bought the Baltimore Bullets with two other investors. It turned out to be a defining moment that would alter each of our lives irrevocably, and eventually, alter the city of Washington, too.

CHAPTER TWO

How clearly I remember the first time we went to the Bullets' home sports facility, the Baltimore Civic Center. As new owners, we drove up to the entrance to the garage and Abe pushed a button. Lo and behold, a monstrous door began lifting up, and we drove inside. I was completely awed. It was huge! I had never been behind the scenes in an arena. As we came in behind and under the seats, ahead of me I could see the brightly lighted area leading onto the basketball floor. My first reaction was, "What have we done?"

What we had done was buy the Baltimore Bullets. That giant door lifting up for us marked our entrance, not only into a huge new building, but into a huge new world. It was very exciting. Growing up in St. Louis, I had been a big fan of our two baseball teams—the Cardinals and the Browns. And since my parents could never afford summer vacations or summer camp, I never left the city in the summer. But I did get tickets from the Knothole Gang through school and I loved going to the baseball games. I always sat in right field, because that's where the tickets were. I became enamored with the players who were in my field of vision: Enos

Slaughter, a right fielder, and Don Gutteridge. I was such an ardent fan that I often waited for my favorite players to emerge after the game so I could get their autographs. They became my heroes. I read everything I could about them.

Many years later, I was getting a view of professional sports from a completely different perspective—the inside. Instead of being thrilled just to get into the stadium and see the players from afar, I was now meeting the players after every game.

I was also learning the day-to-day business of professional sports. How do you put a winning team together? What is the coach's role in developing players and strategies for winning games? What did the other coaches know about your team's strategies and players? How do you keep the game and event exciting enough to keep your fans coming to games, even when the team loses? What are the roles of the general manager and the owner? I loved going to the annual NBA owners' meetings in New York and watching the dynamics of the other owners. How did the commissioner keep those egos from exploding?

I also loved going to the games and getting to know the players afterward. How different it was to be on the inside instead of literally sitting in right field. How different the emotional investment was when you were an owner instead of a fan. And how different the view of the sports media was when you were on the inside seeing what was happening and they were on the outside, criticizing and offering advice, sometimes even implying that the team just didn't want to win. (Why would anyone even be involved in professional sports if he didn't want to win?)

Winning requires many things to come together, so many of which are beyond anyone's control. That is one of the most difficult things you have to accept in professional sports, but it is also what makes it so intriguing; you never know the outcome in advance. That is what motivates owners to buy and run teams and fans to keep coming to the games.

NBA basketball was very different in the late 1960s from what it is today. It was much smaller—only nine teams in the association, compared with thirty today—and each franchise was very small by comparison. When we bought the team, the office in Baltimore was staffed by one employee—Nancy Lacy, who ran the entire show and answered the phone in a cheery, singsong voice: "Bal-ti-more Bullets!"

The Bullets' basketball staff consisted of a general manager and a coach and one or two trainers. Today's staffs consist of hundreds of employees and as many as ten "specialty" coaches.

While it seemed enormous to me at the time, the Baltimore arena was actually quite small, holding only 10,000 seats. Arenas today have twice as many, plus suites and other fan facilities. The relationship between owners and players was also very different. After each home game, we would meet the players in the "Tip In Room" behind the stands to have drinks and to either celebrate a win or commiserate a loss. If the team won, Abe would pass out cigars. The young players looked funny with big cigars in their mouths, but so did my husband; he wasn't the type. In addition to the players and us, there were always groups of attractive young women hanging around at the entrance to the Tip In Room. They were waiting for the players to take them out, which they sometimes did and sometimes didn't. Some had wives and children waiting at home.

We became close to several players and our sons loved being around them after a game and when they occasionally came to our house. We had annual Christmas parties for them at our home in Bethesda.

One year at our party, I was particularly proud of the cake I had decorated as a basketball court. I had the lines drawn on a large sheet cake and had miniature baskets placed at each end. I even found small basketball player figurines in a local variety store and arranged them to appear as though they were playing a game.

I was so proud of this achievement that I asked one of the players, "What do you think?"

"Mrs. Pollin, it looks great except for one thing."

"What is that?" I asked, disappointed.

"Look at the color of the players," he said.

At first I didn't understand what he was telling me, so I looked again. A light bulb went off in my head. They are white! I hadn't even noticed. Most of our players were black, but I just saw them as basketball players, not black ones or white ones.

If anyone had ever asked me if I would like spending the rest of my life in professional sports, I would have thought he or she was crazy. Professional sports? I was interested in music, art, and literature. And, yet, here I was spending two and three nights a week with sports and athletes. I, who had always thought of professional athletes as "brawn rather than brains," was getting to know them. I was learning to respect them in ways I never would have anticipated. One thing I learned was that you couldn't reach that level of professionalism without extraordinary intelligence, and the mental and physical discipline that was required to master the game. Physical prowess was not enough. There were many young boys with incredible physical ability, but it took so much more to make it into the NBA and to stay for an entire career. Some physically talented players are selected to play in the NBA, but their careers may only last three or four years. The players who spent their entire careers—ten or more years—in the NBA were the elite competitors. What an honor it was for me to get to know some of these remarkable young men. I learned a lot from the way they dealt with adversity, whether it was being traded or getting hurt and playing night after night, often in pain. I saw many of them play when they were injured and train ad nauseam in order to get back on the court.

I saw them return after losing a loved one and play their hearts out. I saw their young wives bring their little children to games so they could spend some time as a family. The players during the season were on the road at least two to three days a week. The wives and children knew the drill, but it was a difficult routine for a young family. And that does not include the disappointment of losing. One of the most difficult aspects of the profession was getting traded overnight to another city when you have just purchased your dream house. Professional sports is a very tough business, personally and professionally.

I grew close to many of them and still see some of them and their families.

These players had played and excelled through high school and college basketball, and had learned a lot about how to play and win. But it was in the upper reaches of the NBA that they learned the joys of great wins and the pain of terrible losses. Both of these experiences were described in great detail in the press, by reporters who treated them sometimes as heroes and sometimes as bums. (Also true of the way they treated owners!)

Over the years, we had many colorful players on our team who were fun to be with. Gus Johnson was one. Gus had a gold star embedded in one of his front teeth and a personality that was as bright and dramatic as the star. He was quite good looking, and he knew it. He dressed with flair and often corrected Abe about his clothes. He even offered to dress him, but Abe thought he was a pretty good dresser; he thanked him for the offer and turned him down. When Gus dunked the ball, everyone in the building gasped, so it was not a surprise when he was the first NBA player in history to break the glass backboard. Like all of the NBA players, Gus played to win. At one of our Christmas parties, Abe challenged him to a ping-pong game at the table in our basement. Everyone at the party was watching and Abe beat him. There was a dead silence. Without a word, Gus walked upstairs and out the front door. He not only left the party, he left his wife behind downstairs. Winning was so much a part of his personality that he couldn't tolerate the fact that my husband had beaten him. Especially an "older owner."

Another unique player and NBA superstar with his own special style was Earl "The Pearl" Monroe. Earl had an amazing ability to twist and turn so nobody could guard him on the court. He liked to joke that since *he* didn't know what he was going to do with the ball, the guy guarding him couldn't know either. I developed a fun relationship with Earl. For one of his birthdays, I sent him a black pearl, reminiscent of his nickname. (Recently, he told me that he still had that gift.) Sadly for us, he wanted to be traded to New York instead of playing in Baltimore. It certainly was a sexier city. He fantasized about his perfect future life in the Big Apple, only it never happened. He later said it was one of the biggest mistakes he made in his career. In New York he had to compete with other superstars and never received the kind of attention he got as a Bullet. In fact, some years later when he was inducted into the Basketball Hall of Fame, he chose to wear the Bullets uniform rather than the Knicks.

Becoming friends with some players also had a downside, particularly when or if they were being traded. One of these was Jack Marin, an extremely intelligent young man who planned on going to law school, and did. He would come to the house all the time and we'd talk about everything, including his plans for the future. As so often happens, the team needed to add another player with different skills. When the coaches, general manager, and Abe made that decision, Marin was to be traded for the Houston Rockets' Elvin Hayes, a player we had been watching for years.

Abe and I were both heartsick. How would we tell Jack? We thought he would be devastated. We decided that Abe should meet with Jack to tell him in person to soften the blow. This was unusual. Usually, the player is informed by the coach or general manager, and often he is playing with his new team the following night— sometimes even against his old team.

In a total surprise to us, Jack, it turned out, was more flattered than hurt. "You're trading me for Elvin Hayes? He's a superstar!" he said, "I'm honored. It's a compliment to be traded equally for the 'Big E.'" Rather than sad, we were supposed to be happy for him. His value had been upgraded. Who knew? That's professional sports!

I actually had something to do with our acquiring the "Big E." Elvin Hayes was the one player that I had been watching for years as he played against us. I kept asking Abe how we could get him and his answer always was, "They will never trade him. He's too good."

Standing in a hotel lobby in Seattle on one of our trips, my son Jimmy and I noticed a group of very tall men standing at the other end. One of them broke away and walked over to us. Surprised, as he got closer I recognized him—Elvin Hayes!

"Mrs. Pollin," he said, "I would give anything to play for the Bullets." I was shocked that he knew my name; shocked that he even knew me. I told him that I would relay that information to Mr. Pollin.

As he walked away, Jimmy and I went running off to find Abe, who didn't believe our account at first. But it was true, and that is how Elvin came to the Bullets and helped us win the championship a few years later.

Gradually, I learned more about the science of building a team. It is a highly sophisticated business. You only have a certain number of players, and the key is to get the right fit—players with skill sets that work for the team and personalities that complement each other's and the coach's style of play. It is extremely important, even vital, to get the right match. It is also extremely difficult and rarely happens. (All you have to do is read the sports pages every day to see how hard it is.)

It is also not uncommon to build a team for years that you hope will have that winning combination, only to have the key player get hurt and sit out a year. And all this time, the fans and the media are tracking, hoping and getting disappointed. To succeed in this game, one needs a healthy attitude and a way to deal with frustration. I admire those qualities in all of the players and coaches. The owners have a more complicated road to success; they have to deal with salaries, agents, ticket sales, and sponsors.

I learned over time that you rarely lose track of players you've traded. The NBA is like one big family. Nobody disappears; they just go to another team, which then plays your team, sometimes the following night. It is quite common before the start of the game to watch players from the opposing teams hug and exchange family news. They may even go out together after the game, even though an hour earlier they were beating each other up on the court. Some may play on as many as five or six different teams in the course of their careers. This is true also of coaches and other staff.

You cannot be involved in professional sports and not become passionate, even excessively so, about winning. One time when we were still new owners and on the road with the team in Phoenix, we sat with the owners of the other team on the floor. We thought this would be fun. We liked them as a couple; after all, we shared experiences of being owners. Soon, however, we discovered it was not a good idea. Sitting next to the owner's wife, hearing her yell for her team was too much for me. I wanted to yell for my team! Then, one of her players tripped one of ours, causing him to land hard on the floor. As an owner, one of the first worries is whether your player is hurt and, if he is, how long he will be out. At the moment, I was feeling very angry with her, but then I had to remind myself that she didn't cause him to get hurt. Abe and I really wanted to be friends with this couple, so we never again sat together at a game where our two teams were battling each other.

Another time when I almost lost it in our building was when a woman in the seat in front of me was yelling for the opposite team. She was screaming, jumping up and down, and making nasty remarks about our team. Of course, she had that right. Buy a ticket and you can yell for whoever you want. But I found myself becoming increasingly upset; so upset in fact that, at one point, I couldn't help myself. I watched my right hand moving down toward her ponytail, ready to yank it as hard as I could. Luckily, I came to my senses in time. That would have made for an embarrassing item on the newspaper's sports page: Owner's wife loses it!

Winning and losing—what an emotional roller coaster. The ups and downs are incredible. When we first owned the team, I carried a small bottle of Valium in my handbag. And every time the tension in a game was too much, I'd reach into my handbag, take out the bottle, open it, and take out two tablets—one for me, one for Abe. Without water to make it go down easily, we'd swallow the pills— sometimes more than once a game.

One night in New York, we were playing the New York Knicks—our archrivals—and we lost the game. I was devastated by the loss. When we came back to the hotel room, I threw myself on the bed and began crying uncontrollably. As I was lying there, I realized that this was not behavior that I could continue on a long-term basis. If I was going to be in the sports business, I had to learn how to win and lose and maintain my sanity. I did eventually learn to deal better with the highs and lows, but never completely.

For a time, we became as superstitious as everyone else in the business. For years, our general manager always walked around with a certain number of M&Ms in his pocket for good luck. He would get very upset if the number was wrong. When the Bullets won a game, Abe would wear the same jacket and tie and shoes the next time we played that team. And heaven forbid if he forgot to wear it!

Did it ever work? Who knows? It just felt good!

I've often thought our younger son, Jimmy, should write a book about what it was like to grow up in the world of professional sports. When we first bought the team, Robert was interested in basketball, but was beginning his teens and thus more interested in friends and school activities.

Jimmy was just six, and we brought him to all the games. For some reason we could never figure out, he loved to sit between us in the stands and shout "Boooooo Bullets!" Happily, he stopped doing that after a while. He was always high energy, and we used to let him wander around the stadium on his own. I think he thought of the arena as his second house. Just as the children's book heroine, Eloise, considers New York City's Plaza Hotel her home, so Jimmy considered the Bullets' arena his personal preserve.

He was delighted when some of his favorite players showed up at his bar mitzvah—greatly impressing his friends—but his joy diminished somewhat when he realized everyone was paying attention to the players instead of him! Nonetheless, we have some great pictures of Jimmy holding the Torah, surrounded by all these huge basketball players.

Over time, basketball became a distraction from the tremendous sadness that had overwhelmed us, as Abe and I had hoped it would. There was a gradual sense of easing back into life. For him, it was exciting and challenging. For me, it was also exciting and challenging, but I was not directly involved on a daily basis as he was. I still needed to fill the giant gap my daughter's death had left. I was struggling with her loss and a loss of meaning in my life. I hadn't realized until she died how much of my mental life had been devoted to her for sixteen years. Even while I was caring for my two sons, there was still a huge gap. My sons were healthy and never required the intensive kind of caring and thought that she had.

What could I possibly do that might begin to fill that huge hole? One thought I had was to get a job, get out of the house, have a place I was required to go every day. The problem was I had not worked since my British Army Staff days at age eighteen. I wanted to work, but realized I could only be a volunteer. With the help of a close friend I was able to get a volunteer job at the Peace Corps, counseling returning volunteers. I loved it.

Still, I would often feel the need to pop a Librium each morning as I rode the elevator to my floor. One day, as I was walking out of the side door of my house to go to work, I suddenly had a flash of understanding I'd never had before. I stood at the door, not moving. The feeling was so powerful.

I don't really need to let go of my daughter, I thought to myself. *I just need to learn to live with her memory. I want to hold on to what I had with her, and I can. Her death doesn't mean I have to put the past away. I want her always to be a part of me. I don't want to let go of the memories. They are too beautiful, too precious. I don't want to lose them. And more importantly, I don't HAVE to lose them.*

For me it was as though a bright light had turned on. The light was so bright. Of course, I could live this way. It wouldn't be easy, but I could do it. I stood in the doorway for what seemed forever and then, feeling a rush of relief, I moved around the corner of my house and got into my car. This was a major breakthrough. Nobody, no therapist, had ever presented that option to me.

After that epiphany, I was able to write a letter to her.

> *Dear Lindy Lou,*
>
> *I am writing this final letter to you, honey, a letter that you will never read, but I want so badly to say so many things to you. I've loved you like nothing else in my whole life—such a special love for a special person...my only daughter, my beautiful daughter.*
>
> *Your birthday is approaching, my angel. I swear, Linda, I saw a ring of light around your head the night before you died. You are an angel. I called you that when you were two years old. I can't believe you're not here with me to sit on my bed, telling me you can't fall asleep. "Let's talk, Mom."*
>
> *I miss those talks so much. I miss the look of you, the feel of you. This sounds "corny," I know. That's the word you used in the*

hospital when you said, "I know it's corny, Mom, but would you please hold my hand?"

I would give anything to hold you in my arms.

Somehow, expressing my feelings directly to her helped release some of the powerful emotion that had been building inside of me that otherwise I may not have been able to handle.

For me, the job at the Peace Corps turned out to be the opening to the next phase of my life, just as the Bullets were for Abe. I had never done this before, career counseling; that is, I was corresponding with volunteers overseas to help them transition to returning home, getting jobs, and becoming Americanized again. Often when volunteers returned, they would come to Washington to meet with others and me in the main office. I loved meeting face-to-face with so many of the volunteers I had been corresponding with for months. It was fun and gratifying. In fact, I enjoyed it so much I wanted to move up to a higher position, but I did not have a college degree. I had completed two years at the University of Maryland before getting married, but to advance at the Peace Corps I needed that degree. What would it take? Where and how would I begin at this time of my life? I was 40 years old. What could I handle emotionally, psychologically and physically? I decided to begin slowly by taking some art classes at American University, which was close to my house. I had always been good at drawing. I thought it would be easy and not much of a commitment. I was suffering from dizzy spells and dealing with enormous anxiety. If I needed to miss a class, it wouldn't be a huge loss.

I tried sculpture. I remember the first figure I completed. As I molded the clay into a figure, it almost seemed to flow out of my fingertips. Almost without my thinking, I could feel the figure develop as my hand moved around it.

As my professor walked around the classroom critiquing the student's work he said to me, "You have done this before."

I was surprised. "No," I told him. "Never."

"I don't believe you," he said. "It's too good."

I was pleased and flattered, but totally surprised. I didn't know I could do this.

Then I took my first drawing class and, again, another professor, the head of the art department, Robert D'Arista, said the same thing to me. I didn't realize that I had this talent. I was just able to do it.

Following that, I took painting classes and I learned about color and space. Again, I could really DO it. Amazingly, my first painting was placed in the next department exhibit alongside those of more experienced painters. This could be the beginning of a new and exciting career!

But then something happened that prevented me from continuing.

In art classes, when you complete your work, you turn it around so the class can examine it and critique it. One day when I turned my charcoal drawing of the face of an African-American model and compared it to the drawings of the other students, I discovered something about myself that stunned me.

Her face, the one that I had drawn, looked very different from the ones drawn by others in the class. That is not unusual, except that on mine there was a pained expression on her face. I don't know if the other students in the class noticed this difference, but for me it was a dead giveaway of how I felt. I had no idea how that happened. I had not consciously drawn it that way. The feelings and emotions I was experiencing in my personal life at the time had seeped through my fingers without my knowledge. It frightened me. Again, as in sculpture class, my fingers had spoken for me.

The same was true of a painting that I did of a young girl. Her body language was incredibly revealing of my deepest feelings without my wanting it to be. I knew now that I was seriously depressed, but I did not want everyone in the class to know it. Until then, I had not recognized the profound sadness living inside me. Now it was surfacing in the faces and bodies of the models that I painted and sculpted. It was a truth buried deep inside of me. I didn't want myself revealed like that. These were feelings I had not recognized and they were frightening.

Painting, drawing, and sculpting are solitary activities. Based on the experiences I was having, I decided that I did not want to work alone. I needed to be with people. At this stage of my life, art was too quiet, too lonely, too much with my own thoughts. Even though I felt lucky to have this innate artistic talent, I recognized I needed to find something else as a challenging activity. It was wrong for me now.

One day I got rid of all the painting and sculpting paraphernalia. I carried it downstairs, out of my studio, and put it in my garage. My husband and friends were upset by my decision. "Why are you doing this?" they asked. "You are so good at this!"

I never explained the real reason. I only knew what I felt in my gut. It frightened me to confront this stark truth. I hadn't realized until then how depressed I really was. Having these objects that I had created staring back at me, telling me how I felt inside, was something I could not ignore, something I would have to deal with—but not yet.

The doorbell rang early one evening, and when I opened it, my sister Betty was standing outside looking bedraggled and frightened.

"Betty, what are you doing here?" I asked, my heart pounding as I stepped aside to let her in.

"I thought I'd visit."

"How did you get here?"

"I just walked out," she said, "No one was looking, so I just walked out. I know my way around Washington. I know how to get here." She shrugged. "I just came."

The institution that was supposed to be caring for Betty wasn't. She snuck out.

This was not the first time; it was happening frequently. This became yet another nightmare for me. The woman who kept coming to my doorstep was a constant reminder that my beautiful, talented, loving sister was no longer, just like all the other important people who had been in my life and left. If Betty coming to our house was upsetting, it was nothing like my recurrent fear that something terrible would happen to her one of the times she walked out and didn't come to my house, but instead wandered around the streets of Washington. Would I get a phone call one night from the police telling me that they found my baby sister dead in some alley?

Betty's husband, Jack, was caring for Ilene and Howard, but gave up all responsibility in caring for Betty. My parents were dead. Betty's children had been so young when she first was institutionalized, they had no real memory of her. That left me as her only surviving relative.

Reaching a point of no return can occur at the oddest times and in the oddest places. "I don't think I can keep doing this," I told Abe one evening in the car as we were on our way out to dinner.

"I just have the feeling that it's going to be me or her," I blurted out. I simply couldn't hold it in any longer. I felt that I was at the stage of breaking. I needed help.

After much searching, I accidentally found the place my sister was to spend the rest of her life. An old boyfriend of my sister's and his wife, Robert and Joy Cohen, founded a series of group homes. Fortunately, for Betty and for me, it was a secure and loving place. This was the help that allowed me to live without the ongoing worry of what would happen to my sister. I was able to finally feel secure knowing she was safe. Now, I could try to move on with my life.

=============

In addition to my mind, my body was sending me additional signals that something was wrong. I was dizzy for an entire year, and no doctor could figure out the cause. I never fell, but there were many times when I had to hold on to a wall to keep steady. Often when friends invited us out I had to cancel at the last minute. I couldn't watch television. I couldn't read. I went to doctor after doctor in Washington, and although I didn't learn what my problem was, I learned something about doctors' networks. One doctor would refer me to another doctor, but each time the new doctor looked at the diagnosis of the first doctor, and he would agree with it. *Some kind of inner ear problem.* Nobody came up with anything new, and the old diagnosis didn't seem to lead to recovery. I wasn't in pain. I was ostensibly strong and healthy, but I couldn't do anything. I had basically shut down. Many days I would go to art class and in the middle call someone to take me home. Also, at this time, I began to have back pain, and again the doctors were unable to give me a diagnosis or treatment. I spent many hours—whole days—lying on a sofa with my legs up on a high pillow.

As depressed as I was, these mysterious physical symptoms were about to destroy whatever was left of my life. I couldn't attend my children's school or sports activities. I mostly sat at home trying to figure out how I could get out of this horrible, seemingly unending, situation. My husband was wonderful, supportive, and sympathetic, but he was also stumped. I particularly remember a nurse in the ear, nose, and throat doctor's office, yelling at me over the phone, "I told you not to bend over the waste basket!" I put the phone down and cried until there were no tears left. Who could help me?

I kept asking myself, what do I have to do to get through this?

After a year with no relief, I decided to go to the famous Mayo Clinic in Minnesota. They were supposed to be excellent diagnosticians. I was ready to try anything. Abe and I stayed at a hotel with an underground tunnel that went directly into the clinic building. I needed to hold on to the wall each day as I walked through the tunnel with Abe holding my other hand.

What was wrong with me?

The clinic routine was excellent. A new patient goes through a thorough, three-day diagnostic procedure. The staff was made up of wonderfully warm and welcoming Midwesterners. I immediately felt at home. Naturally, I was quite nervous, but the first doctor I saw made me feel very comfortable. He began from the beginning, asking every possible question about my life, and yes, there had been sixteen years of almost nonstop trauma--all with tragic endings. He listened carefully and thoughtfully, and followed the protocol of beginning anew. When I had called to make the appointment, I asked if they wanted my records and they said, "No, we like to start fresh." That was the best news I had heard in a year.

After several hours of questioning, the doctor asked me to sit on the examining table. Then he gently handed me a small, brown paper bag—the kind you used to get in the grocery store when you were buying candy. He said, "Breathe into the bag."

I thought he was kidding. I said, quite sarcastically, "I came all the way to the famous Mayo Clinic, and you're asking me to breathe into a paper bag?"

"Just breathe into the bag," he said, smiling.

So I did. After all, I hadn't come all this distance not to follow the doctor's orders. So as soon as I began filling the bag with my breath, I began to experience familiar dizzy symptoms. I almost fell off the table, but the doctor was smiling. I felt foolish, but he just helped me off the table. He said he would see me in a few days after they had completed the rest of the tests to get the results. In the interim, he would consult with the other specialists. I felt that I had finally come to the right place. They would be able to help me.

After several days of tests, I met again with the original physician. The results showed me to be healthy and strong; nothing wrong. I was thrilled to hear the good news, but why was I still dizzy? The doctor said, "Go home and play tennis."

"Play tennis? Are you kidding? How can I play tennis when I can't walk straight?"

"You are hyperventilating," he said. "The tension in your body is causing you to breathe faster than normal. That is causing your body to be low in carbon dioxide, which constricts the blood vessels, preventing the transport of oxygen. And that is making you dizzy."

I was extremely pleased to hear I didn't have something serious, but I still didn't know what to do. This was a problem that would not go away and was causing me to lose extremely valuable time in my life. I had already lost so much of that.

"So what do I do?" I asked.

"Exercise will help, anything that will reduce stress," he said. "Go home and be with your husband and children and relax. You'll be fine."

I left feeling dizzy, but grateful for the diagnosis. All I had to do was to find a way to reduce stress. I still didn't know what to do. How do you reduce stress?

A friend suggested yoga. She said that it was good for breathing exercises. This was the 1970s, and few people did yoga in the United States. It was strange and exotic. But I was desperate to try anything that would help me live a normal life again. I tried several yoga classes, but they were more about strange positions with hyper Indian teachers. And then I found George, a yoga instructor who came to the house.

When George, in his orange jumpsuit, pulled up on his motorcycle in front of my house, I wondered what my neighbors would think. George was a serious yoga pupil and teacher. He also played the flute.

"Look, George," I said. "Before we begin I want to tell you what I need. I don't want to do anything but breathe. I don't want to do headstands or complicated twists. I just want to learn to breathe."

He was perfectly willing to do as I wished. The first few times I could hardly keep from giggling while I was lying on the carpet in a guest bedroom. The tape recorder was playing flute music recorded in the Taj Mahal while I was halfheartedly trying to breathe the way he told me. It all seemed silly.

After several sessions, I told myself to stop fighting. I gave in and began breathing according to his instructions, difficult as it was. After struggling for about a half hour, my entire body started to shake involuntarily. My arms and legs flailed uncontrollably, and tears I couldn't stop rolled down my face.

It was frightening. Was I losing control? I tried to understand what was happening. What was happening was a massive release of all of the years of fear, anxiety, loss, and tension. I had been holding everything inside of me. My entire body had become tight as a drum and I hadn't realized it. What a revelation! What a release and a relief!

That marked the beginning of four years of yoga with George and a lifetime of paying attention to my body and what it was telling me. Years later, in my office between patients, I would sometimes close the door, lie down on the floor and do some stretching and breathing. Even now I do breathing exercises before getting out of bed in the morning. When I do it, I realize that even though I thought I had slept well, my body had been in fact tense the entire night. Understanding what my body is feeling has helped me enormously over the years. I now automatically check my level of body tension. If it is getting high, I immediately do something to reduce it—walk, stretch, breathe, or swim. I had lived a major part of my life being unaware of the tension I was holding in. I am forever grateful to George, wherever he is.

==============

In addition to art classes at American University, I also had begun anthropology classes just because I was fascinated by the subject. I think it was a throwback to my early years in St. Louis, when I longed to travel and know about exotic places around the world. I needed a major to get a degree, so I decided to major in cultural anthropology. There I was, in my forties, spending my days with long-haired, open-sandaled, highly-politicized 1970s college students, and in the evenings going to Bullets basketball games as an owner. The contrast in my daily activities was rather great, to say the least, but it actually became the pattern for the rest of my life.

I was fascinated by cultural anthropology. If I hadn't met Abe when I did, I might have traveled the world, even lived in some exotic place for a time. Of course, I was not only too old to become an anthropologist, I had a family and an existence that didn't make it possible. But that didn't stop me from fantasizing.

Within cultural anthropology, I became particularly interested in African studies and took many courses in it. I loved learning about the various tribes and their customs, their movements across the continent. I learned their art works and even their physical distinctions. In 1973, Abe and I began planning a trip. I suggested we visit East Africa. Luckily, he agreed and I loved him for it. I couldn't believe it. I was actually going to be in Africa, in person.

We arranged to travel by private car with our own driver. This allowed us to be free to wander and change our plans as we wished. Our first stop was Kampala, Uganda. As we stepped down from the plane, we heard a strange loud sound. It was a group of women meeting the plane, chanting a welcome with a strange clicking sound. What a way to arrive in Africa!

Through our Israeli friends in Washington, we had been introduced to people at the Embassy in Kampala. As luck would have it, there was a reception being held the night we arrived, which we attended. Because many of the staff had been in Uganda for some time, I took the opportunity to ask what would be an exciting and unusual place to visit. One woman seemed to understand that we were looking for a special experience and suggested we visit an isolated area in the northeastern corner of Uganda where there was a primitive tribe called the Karamojong.

It meant that we would have to adjust our plans, but our driver was game. Before we left Kampala, the arrangements were made. This was the real thing; the chance of a lifetime. The only problem was that it required us to travel by small plane deep into a remote area and I was terrified of small planes. What was I to do? Struggling with my decision, I realized I wanted to go there more than I was afraid.

A few days later when we got to Nairobi, we hired a single plane. "Are you sure you want to go to there?" the British pilot, in his crisply starched khaki uniform, asked us. "I can take you to the beach!"

"No," we said. "We can go to the beach any time. That is where we want to go!"

The next day we flew in a tiny, single-engine airplane over miles and miles of the starkest, most barren land I had ever seen. Looking down, there was literally nothing to see. Our pilot had never seen this before either. He was searching for a place to land, and a marker to let us know when we arrived. But because there were no landmarks—no cows, no crops, no roads, nothing, just bare trees—we flew around in circles for a long time. Finally, he spotted a little outhouse. That was the marker that told us where to land.

A tall dark-haired Englishman in a jeep met us and took us to the village of the Karamojong tribe. The man had gone there years before on an aid mission for a British organization and stayed, building a house in this extremely remote area. As we approached the village, we saw clay huts and twenty or thirty women waiting for us with a group of young children. Their skins were very dark and shiny, and the women were bare breasted. They were wearing layer upon layer of necklaces, and I felt that I had stepped into a photograph in *National Geographic* magazine. There was something

I had never seen, even in a photograph. The men were naked except for penis covers. I could not believe my eyes.

As I stepped from the jeep, the women surrounded me and began touching my hair. They had never seen blond hair. The Brit told me they thought I was brought there to be his wife. As they became accustomed to our presence, they became friendly. One woman invited me to enter her mud hut. I was scared, but also flattered that she invited me. Not knowing what I would find inside, but not wishing to hurt her feelings, I bent down and crawled in. I was completely taken aback. It was spotless. There was a mud floor packed down hard, but shiny clean. There were no utensils or anything else in the small space. I was on my knees looking around me, and she examined my expression, looking for my response. I could see how proud she was of the way it looked inside. It clearly pleased her that I had come into her spotless home. We shook hands as I left.

To have this experience our first week in Africa was unbelievable. This was a tribe I had never heard of. The Englishman's living room was stacked with dozens of their masks and shields. We bought a few from him, but never received them after we returned home. I am sure he was quite surprised when, a few years later, my husband went back there on a trip for UNICEF. Abe was quite amused at the destination he'd been assigned. "Hardly anyone ever goes there once," he said. "And here I am going twice!"

I had an unusual experience when we visited Queen Elizabeth National Park, our first national park in Uganda, several hundred miles southwest of Kampala. We arrived in the evening and went to bed early so we could be up first thing in the morning to see the animals. I was also so pleased with the way I'd packed for this three-week trip. Polyester clothes had just come into fashion, and I had brought with me two pairs of navy knit pants that could easily be washed and dried overnight. While my husband was relaxing on one of the twin beds in the room, I washed my pants (I am a little obsessive) and put them out on the balcony rail to dry.

As I stood on the balcony in the quiet darkness, looking at the clearest sky I had ever seen and the full moon shining overhead, I was filled with the excitement of being in Africa. I heard the sounds of animals in the distance. The sounds grew louder and louder, when suddenly a dark figure jumped up in front of me on the other side of the rail—a human being. I froze. Before I could speak, he grabbed my newly washed knit pants, jumped off the balcony and ran off into the darkness. When I caught my breath, I screamed to Abe, who was relaxing in the bedroom, "Honey, a man just took my pants! Quick, go get him!"

"Are you kidding?" he said. "I'm not going out after him in the dark!"

"But my pants!" I cried.

To this day I laugh when I think about the man in Uganda running around in a pair of ladies' navy blue polyester pants.

Thanks to me, Abe also had an extraordinary experience. As was typical, I often pushed him into activities he didn't particularly want to do, but did anyway. I think he knew that these would be stories he could tell when he got home. They were.

Barney, a friend at the American Embassy, invited him to go shooting. Not only had Abe never used a gun, he had barely ever seen one. But off he went in the dark early morning to meet Barney, who was an experienced hunter. Back home later that night and exhausted, Abe reported that they went out in a fully equipped elephant-hunting vehicle filled with a variety of guns and equipment. Also along was Barney's thirteen-year-old son. He said that they accidentally killed the wrong animal. After almost being run down by a pride of elephants, Barney had accidentally killed a female springbok. This was not done. Abe said he had never been so terrified in his entire life. I felt guilty for urging him to go, but he did have this story that he loved to tell for the rest of his life.

From there, we drove out to the bush to find animals--and we found them. It was incredibly exciting to see lions asleep in the shade of the trees with their cubs hugging them, and cheetahs chasing predatory animals away from their babies.

From Nairobi, we went to the Ngorongoro Crater in Tanzania, a cauldron-like volcanic feature that has one of the densest concentrations of wildlife in all of Africa. We drove down the side of the crater in a small jeep to the bottom, where we saw a flock of magnificent pink flamingos. We also saw many other species of birds and animals that could not be found anywhere else in the world. This time we traveled with a few people and a guide who, when we reached the bottom, suggested we take care of any toilet needs before we continued. "Just over there, beyond that big boulder," he said. I thought, "how clever" that the government had maintained a "natural look" with a boulder in front of the ladies' room just like the parks out west in our country. But as I walked around, I realized the boulder *was* the ladies' room. What was I supposed to do? What choice did I have? I would just have to crouch down. And if that wasn't enough of a new experience for a city girl who had never even been camping, when I crouched down I found myself staring into the eyes of a huge warthog, a wild member of the pig family! He stared at me and I stared back until he slowly walked away This was Africa! It fulfilled all of my dreams.

The most exciting part of that trip was seeing the great migration in Tanzania—millions of wild animals of every species traveling to new watering holes. Springbucks (a deer species) were literally jumping over the front of our car. We got to see hundreds of zebras, elephants and other species running on both sides of the road with their babies. There were very few tourists in Africa then, and we were literally the only car on the road. It was a thrill we never forgot, driving mile after mile in the midst of the thunderous sounds of the animals' hoofs and clouds of dust they created. We looked from one window to the next wanting to catch and hold the memory in our heads.

When we returned to our lodge that evening, I was relaxing before dinner when Abe came running to our room to tell me that he had just made a new friend, one of the tribal chiefs. He wanted me to meet him. I ran out, and there was a tall, handsome, young man wearing only an orange blanket. Abe invited him to have a drink with us in the lodge dining room, which he accepted. We sat in front of a roaring fire (it was cool at night) waiting for our drinks. When Abe had asked him what he would like, he said he would have what we were having. So Abe ordered three scotch and sodas, while I was wondering what I needed to do in order not to see what was under his blanket. When the drinks came and he tasted his, he spit it out. He said that beer is the drink of the Masai. He didn't like the scotch and soda.

After we spent an hour talking with our driver acting as translator, he said he had to get back to his village. Abe asked how he would manage. It was getting dark. How would he deal with the wild animals on the way? He told Abe not to worry. He was wearing magical beads around his neck. If he felt he was in trouble, all he had to do was to bite down on them and he would be safe. Even though he promised to meet us the following morning, we never saw him again.

Like the accidental opportunity to visit the Karamojong tribe, on the way to our next destination I asked our driver if we were near the Ituri Rainforest in the Congo. Amazingly, he said yes. Again, I asked if it would be possible for us to go there, and he said yes. "We can do it in a day," he said. "In fact, we can do it now, if you wish." Did I wish?

Looking over at Abe to see his response, all I saw was a big smile, "Let's go!" Did I ever love this guy. Turning the car around, we crossed the border from Kenya to Congo and were on our way into a dark, dense forest. I was in seventh heaven. Within an hour, we approached a clearing where there were thirty Mbuti pygmies in the midst of some sort of ceremony. We couldn't believe our eyes. To the right of our car, they were dancing in a circle around a fire. Seeing our car, they waved us down and invited us to join them, which we did, of course.

Standing next to them, we felt like giants. They were all less than five feet tall. Later, when we drove off, three jumped onto the hood of the car to lead us out of the forest. I learned something quite interesting. As our car approached a more open area, one of them pointed to what he thought was an ant. But it wasn't an ant; it was a car in the distance. Our driver explained: because they live in a dense environment, they cannot judge distance. They don't have perspective; they never see a view from a distance. I couldn't wait to get back to my African studies class and tell everyone about our adventures. I had met members of the various tribes we had studied. I thought my professor would be thrilled that I had had this opportunity and would want to hear all my stories. Instead, her response was cool. I could not understand it, but she was not interested. A year later after I graduated, I learned why.

==============

I was not the same person I had been before Linda died. I had been fulfilled as a mother and wife. Abe and I had a satisfying social life with friends from the time we were married, some in the same business and community activities, sharing our children as they arrived and grew. I hadn't longed for a career or other life. I loved being a wife, a mother and Abe's partner in our business.

We had endured the devastating loss of two children, but after Linda's death I had a huge emptiness. I hadn't realized how much of my time was spent making sure her life went as normally as possible. Old friends were supportive and caring, but I no longer identified with them.

The friends we had before no longer fit my different sense of self, the change in our business world and our place in the

Washington community. Many close women friends invited me to lunch or shopping to be supportive, but I found such get-togethers unsatisfying. Rather than cheer me up as they had hoped, they made me sad. While they talked about their children, all I could do was close my mind and smile.

When one worried about her son's upcoming tonsillectomy, all I could do was refrain from making a comparison to my children's heart operations and then their loss. They could not know how I felt and I could not tell them. I did not want to hurt their feelings and I also did not want to reveal mine.

I began to realize I needed to spend time with people who could understand my state of mind, who had a better sense of my feelings of loss, grief, and mourning. My husband was wonderful and tried to be my whole family, but I could not depend completely on him. He was also struggling and needed support. In times like this, marriages often fail because the husband and wife don't realize he or she needs more support than the other can give.

My number of women friends became quite limited; few were able to fulfill my huge need for understanding. I was depressed and needy. I was extremely grateful for one long-time friend, Cherry Adler. She seemed to have no limit to the love and understanding she was able to give me. Around this time, Abe and I went to a party in our neighborhood. Except for the host, we had never met any of these people. This event opened up a new group of friends for us. We met Bob Pierpoint, the White House correspondent for CBS News, and his wife Pat, and connected with them immediately. Bob and Abe began to play tennis, and the four of us developed a deep and lasting friendship. Not only did we see them often, they also introduced us to their media friends—a very different world for us. I believe now it helped that they'd had no connection with us prior to Linda's death. Instead of being reminders of the past, they offered us a different and new future. They became our closest friends. Washington is a divided city. Those in the world of government, politics, diplomacy, and journalism rarely cross paths with the local business community. Through the Pierpoints, we met their reporter friends—correspondents Marvin and Bernie Kalb and Dan Karasik, who worked with Bob at CBS; White House correspondents from other networks like NBC's Herb Kaplow; Marvin Stone, who was editor-in-chief of *U.S. News & World Report*, and his wife, Terry. When we got together for dinner—usually at Dan and Lois Karasik's—we would spend a fun and exciting evening listening to them poke fun at some of the politicians they covered. In Washington, the media is both king and the source of all kinds of interesting information. Our large parties and small dinners were always lively. Whether we were at a Bullets game or at someone's home, gossiping was central. We always laughed, too, which is what we needed after so much pain and sorrow. We loved being with them.

In 1974, we took a trip to Hong Kong. Bernie Kalb suggested we meet a friend of his, Ted Koppel, who was working in the area. We were traveling by ferry and arranged to meet on the dock. We arrived early, and only one person was there: a very young-looking guy with a strange mass of curly blond hair. We dismissed the possibility that this kid was the man we were meeting. He was too young to be a foreign correspondent in Vietnam.

We looked him over.

He looked us over.

Finally, he walked over to us and said, "Are you the Pollins?"

Abe suspiciously looked at him. "Are you Ted Koppel?"

Years later, we always laughed about the incident because we were both expecting very different looking people. Ted had been told that Abe was the owner of a basketball team, and he was looking for an old fat man with a cigar. We were told that Koppel was an established foreign correspondent, so we also expected a wrinkled, worn-out looking reporter. Talk about prejudging people!

That evening with Ted and his wife, Grace Anne, marked the beginning of a very long and dear friendship, partly because of a phone call that I had received a few hours earlier in our hotel room. I had just learned that my application to the University of Maryland graduate school in social work had been turned down. I had been counting on going to graduate school. I was terribly disappointed. My grades at American University were excellent. I could not understand why I wasn't accepted.

At dinner, I found myself confiding in Grace Anne. She insisted I call the school when I got back and find out why I had been rejected. She said I had a right to know and they had an obligation to tell me. I had no idea how her advice would change my life.

When we returned, I made an appointment with the Dean of the School. He was very gracious. He told me that I'd been rejected because my cultural anthropology professor, who'd given me very high marks, had not endorsed me. He could not understand why I asked her to write a letter of recommendation. I had no clue as to her feelings about me. I was shocked.

He then accepted me into the school, but I had already applied to Catholic University and been accepted. It was the best "bad thing" that ever happened to me. But, for years, I tried to understand why she had done that. What did I miss?

The only reason I ever came up was her "cool" response when I'd returned from Africa. Perhaps she was envious I was able to make the kind of trip she couldn't. I never found out, but I lost some of my naiveté as a result of the experience. People who are jealous can do evil things; she tried to hurt me in her small way.

Two years later, I was asked to serve on the American University's Board of Directors. Attending my first meeting, the professor who had written the rejection letter was sitting in the row facing me. I still remember the look on her face.

This experience was one of the first I had where someone resented me and I had not recognized it. I believe she saw me as the privileged wife of a wealthy businessman and professional sports team owner—a rich woman who could afford a trip she couldn't.

I saw myself as an excited student, eager to find something worthwhile in my life again. It was an issue that would come back to haunt me time and again.

===============

Our ties to Israel were deep. Abe's parents were long-time supporters of the State of Israel, and along with them we supported every fundraising dinner and event. Abe loved to describe one particular event to anyone who would listen. In 1945, soon after World War II, his father announced he was taking him downtown to a meeting. When Abe asked where, his father couldn't tell him. "You'll see."

They went to an office building where a Middle Eastern-looking guy was standing guard at the door. He and others in the room were from the Haganah, the Jewish military organization fighting for Israel's creation. With them were about 20 leaders of the Washington Jewish community. The door was locked and the group was told, "Nobody leaves here until we raise the money."

They raised the money. The next morning they bought an old steamship in Baltimore and renamed it Exodus. It was put to use to smuggle Holocaust survivors from Europe into what was then pre-Israel Palestine. At the time, Palestine was under British rule and a British blockade prohibited Holocaust survivors from entering Israel. The publicity Exodus and other similar vessels received caused the British to turn Palestine over to the United Nations, which then voted to allow the creation of a Jewish state.

Abe was very proud of having participated in this event. Whenever he told the story, he described himself as a "kid," but actually we were already married. I believe he felt like a kid among these pillars of the Jewish community.

Through the tradition started by Abe's father, we also became supporters of Israel. As a result, we took our first trip to Israel in 1961, when the nation was still very young. Harry Brager was a good friend of ours at the time, and he worked for the Israel Bond Office in Washington. Each time he took a trip to Israel, he urged us to go. He was completely taken with what was happening in Israel and wanted to share it with us. We had just built our house in Bethesda, so our answer was always, "Harry, we need to furnish our new house first!"

He would not take no for an answer. One evening, in our barely furnished den, he marched to the phone on the table next to the sofa, dialed a couple of numbers, and next, we heard him make plane and hotel reservations. He made the decision for us, and we never regretted it.

Arriving at the airport outside of Tel Aviv, we saw Harry calling to us through the open window of a one-story, unpainted wooden building. He had arranged for us to stay on the beach in the first motel ever built in Israel with a pool and air-conditioning.

Harry made sure we had experiences we could never have had on our own. We went to factories, kibbutzim, and army posts in addition to the ancient sites. Seeing Jews from every part of the world—places we'd never known had Jewish populations, like North Africa, Southern Russia, the Middle East, India, and China—was thrilling. We saw women from Kurdistan wearing colorful native costumes, people of every skin color, Jews separated for centuries now living together for the first time ever. With my love of cultural anthropology, I could not get over the fact that I had never known these people existed and had maintained their Jewish identity in whatever part of the world in which they lived.

At this time, the country was still quite undeveloped; there was no luxury. Women working in the kibbutz begged me to send them American cosmetics. Simple things like Pepto-Bismol tablets were unknown.

We had long conversations over healthy Israeli salads. Many Army officers advised us, "Buy land in Israel. You never know what is going to happen." The memories of what had happened in Europe were still fresh. Our only other tie to Israel was through our decision after Linda died to support a young Israeli woman's university education. We did this through the Israeli Embassy in Washington, and had met a counselor there, Ephraim Levy, and his wife, Malca. That led to a whole new circle of friends—the Israeli diplomats. Because Malca was a terrific cook, the Levys had lots of dinner parties in their small apartment. Usually, the parties were Abe and I and another couple. Other people would show up, quite casually. These people, both Americans and Israelis, never stayed the whole evening. They would come and go, sometimes after spending a short time, gathering in the kitchen. Many of the Americans who came "worked at the White House." Others, like Jim Angleton, who came regularly, used to invite the Levys to his farm in Wisconsin to see his orchid collection. He also "did work for the government."

Years later, it was revealed that Jim Angleton had been head of counterintelligence at the CIA and had helped set up Mossad, Israel's intelligence agency. We realized we had spent many wonderfully engaging evenings at the Levys surrounded by both American and Israeli spies. What's more, we had been there to provide the cover, to be part of what appeared to be a dinner party that enabled men to stroll in and out, clustering in the kitchen to exchange information with their contacts, without attracting attention. We were so naïve. We just enjoyed the good company and good food, never grasping the true purpose of the evenings.

Many, many years later, long after the Levys returned to Israel, they came back to the United States for a visit. I confronted Ephraim. "Tell me the truth. Were you a spy?" He looked at Malca and laughed. "Yes, I was," he replied. Totally oblivious to what was going on right under our noses, Abe and I had wonderful times with the Levys, eating Malca's delicious food and enjoying the company of the many Israelis they entertained—kibbutzniks and war heroes in addition to spies.

The late 1960s and early 1970s were a very good time for Israel. The Six-Day War had ended victoriously, and the Israeli diplomatic corps consisted of many young people who were emblematic of the vibrant young Israel that was emerging.

No one was more representative of the New Israel than the man who was Israel's Ambassador to the United States: Yitzhak Rabin. Rabin had commanded the Israel Defense Forces that had miraculously managed to achieve victory over Egypt, Syria, and Jordan in the Six-Day War. He was a much acclaimed war hero. His wife, Leah, was star material on her own, having served with her husband as part of the secret commando unit of the pre-state, underground Jewish army.

One fall night in 1968, we were at our usual small casual dinner, and the Levys' doorbell rang late in the evening. We all went to the door to greet Yitzhak and Leah. Leah was still wearing her full-length mink coat. It was a perfect entrance for this couple, which would make such an impact on the world.

We soon learned that Leah loved to play tennis and Yitzhak would go along. Abe and I also played tennis, with me going along, but we did have a tennis court in our back yard. This made for some wonderful opportunities. We began playing doubles at our house and having lunch together afterward. Abe was a very good tennis player, as was Leah. Yitzhak was okay, and I was mediocre. (During many a game I could hear Abe's voice behind me, "Out of my way!" which I was glad to oblige.)

Through many tennis games, lunches at our house, and dinner parties Leah hosted at the Ambassador's residence, the four of us began a close friendship that would last until Yitzhak's untimely death. We spent much time together, both at large embassy parties and just the four of us sitting around. We became close enough to talk about everything—what was going on in Israel as well as in Washington. We spent many evenings at the Israeli Embassy, and Yitzhak and Leah became Bullets fans (although he slept through a few games).

What brought me particularly close to Leah was a gesture she made early in our relationship. Somehow, early on, she had learned about Linda's death. One day when we met for lunch, she gave me a translation of a beautiful Israeli poem; a poem about losing a child. She understood particularly because she also had a daughter with a heart condition that fortunately was not serious. I was deeply touched, and never forgot this sensitive and generous gesture.

She was a tremendous asset to Yitzhak. Since his English was not very good when he arrived in the U.S., she wrote all his speeches and stepped in to speak as needed. She was a sophisticated hostess and a wonderful cook. She had learned from her mother, who was a caterer in Israel. Dinners at the embassy were always excellent. Also being artistically sophisticated, she filled the embassy walls with wonderful new Israeli art. They were a close couple and often played off each other. Whereas he was shy, she had strong opinions, a love of gossip and no hesitation in speaking up. It was not unusual when we were sitting together in a room, I could hear Yitzhak's deep baritone voice cautioning her, "Leah…LEAH!" He would giver her a look and she'd back off. They complemented each other beautifully.

Even though Yitzhak was an excellent statesman, he was reserved in social situations. One of the reasons I got to know him as well as I did was that Leah always put me at his side at dinner parties. He always felt comfortable with me and I could make him laugh.

Leah and I spent a lot of time together, often just the two of us. One day we were having lunch in the sunroom in my house, laughing and talking, when she became quite serious. She wasn't usually so forthcoming, but this time she poured out her feelings between tears. This was very unusual behavior for her. She took pride in being tough, resilient, and noncommittal.

I was surprised at what had upset her. There had been a

luncheon for other ambassadors' wives and she had not been invited. Not being a part of the diplomatic community, I was not aware that there were several different diplomatic clubs and Israel had been excluded from them all. Was it anti-Semitism? Was it because Israel was such a new state? Was it political? She could not understand it and neither could I. I stared across the table at this strong, dynamic, intelligent, gifted woman whose eyes were filled with tears. I couldn't think of a reason any club would exclude her. I learned two things about Leah Rabin that day: she had a vulnerable side, and she was not accustomed to being excluded.

It was not long, however, before she gained acceptance!

Through the Rabins, we also became close friends of Yael and Amos Eiran, both of whom worked at the Israeli Embassy. Amos eventually became Yitzhak's chief of staff when Yitzhak became prime minister.

On Yitzhak's fiftieth birthday, the six of us went to the Eirans' apartment to celebrate. I gave Yitzhak a small statue I'd found of a little boy sitting on a rock, fishing, with a note that said "Men never grow up." He loved it. After he died, Leah told me it never left his desk. The six of us were fortunate to have been able to know each other in this way.

==============

Abe didn't really like doing things in partnership. He liked being his own man. He liked to say that I was his only partner, and frankly I think he preferred that I be a relatively silent partner. When the Bullets had a particularly bad year in 1968 and the fans started staying away, the men with whom we'd bought the team, Arnold Heft and Earl Foreman, wanted out. At first they persuaded Abe to accept an offer from a Boston group that would move the franchise to Miami. After tossing and turning a couple of nights, Abe decided he couldn't do it.

"Why should I give up my passion—something I love—

for money?" he asked me. Based on the Boston offer, he offered to buy out his partners and take over sole possession of the ball club. They agreed to the terms, but what followed was kind of amusing.

The all-male world of NBA basketball can get terribly macho about silly things. Guys will be guys, and guys love to win games, even very little ones. We'd negotiated a number for the buyout that everyone agreed to, and the next thing I knew, we were going to meet with Earl and Arnold and their wives in a conference room to close the deal. We sat down at a huge, completely bare conference table. Abe and I sat down on one side of the table. They sat down on the other side of the table. We'd brought the check with us, and Abe placed the check on the table.

Nothing happened. No one picked it up. There we were, sitting in silence at the big, bare table, staring at the one little piece of paper in the middle. For the longest time, no one moved. Who would pick up it up? Finally, when the tension in the room couldn't get any higher, Arnold's wife slowly reached out and slid the check close to her. The standoff had ended. Abe and I became the sole owners of the Baltimore Bullets.

That year things picked up enormously. The Bullets drafted Wes Unseld, who became Rookie of the Year and Most Valuable Player. We also ended up winning the division. However, it did not alter the financial problems. People in Baltimore weren't coming to games.

A sports team has to be an integral part of a community, and even though Abe and I tried for five years to engage Baltimore, it never happened. We invited local politicians, business people, and celebrities to games, but the city never responded. Attendance was falling off, and revenues were falling off, too.

By 1972 the money losses had increased and we felt we had two choices: sell the team or move the team out of Baltimore. Again, as far as Abe was concerned, the first wasn't really an option.

We decided to move the team to Washington, something we had long considered, ideally to a building where we could be tenants. But there was no such building, and Washington was in bad financial shape. No one in the city government could even consider building a building or investing in one. Again, Arnold Heft, our former partner, called Abe and told him about a piece of property that was available. It wasn't exactly in the center of town, but it was on the Washington Beltway.

Looking at it for the first time, we found a swamp in a totally desolate area. Our car got stuck in the mud. Okay, so it wasn't our first choice. But looking on the bright side, it *was* on the Washington Beltway—and thus both accessible and in the Washington area. Because there was nothing else around, there would be plenty of space to build both a big arena and lots of parking. We didn't have a lot of choices and this is where we were going to move.

Next came the exciting part for both Abe and me. We had years of construction experience behind us, but this was a new kind of building. The challenge was to know what it needed to be. Fortunately, we had been in sports for ten years. But this was to become a major entertainment center. We had built apartment buildings, but not buildings to house circuses. This building had to handle rock concerts, ice shows, wrestling matches, horse shows, and hockey games. In Washington, it would even have to handle presidential galas. Washington had never had such a facility.

The excitement was palpable as two construction people, Jim Clark from George Hyman Construction and Albert Cohen, joined Abe and me on an unforgettable, one-day trip around the country to look at the newest arenas. Our first stop was Minneapolis, then San Francisco, and finally Houston.

Even though everyone knew construction, no one had ever built an arena. In each building, we asked millions of questions. Now we had to think about the many different needs the building would have to fill. We asked the managers in each city what they would do differently if they were going to build a new building. What mistakes did they make? How would they correct them if they had the chance? "How tall are those doors?" I asked the people in San Francisco. (After all, if we were going to have circuses, the doors would have to be high enough to accommodate elephants!)

While the men were sitting on the plane, looking over the building plans, I began staring out of the window, trying to figure out a name for this new building. It was in the Washington area, but not in Washington.

National Arena? The Nation's Arena? The Capital Arena?

I came up with "Capital Centre." After all, the building would be the center of sports entertainment in the capital of the United States. Everyone on the plane loved it, and that was it.

We returned from the trip with a host of excellent ideas, but another problem. To bring in enough revenue, we had to have another professional sports team playing a full season. That would be a professional ice hockey team.

That year, 1972, was big. The next thing I knew, Abe and I were in Montreal at the annual meeting of the National Hockey League in hopes of winning a franchise. Abe had been chairman of the NBA's expansion committee two years earlier and he knew a lot about franchises. Still, looking over the scene in Montreal, we decided we needed some reinforcements. Our immediate adviser was always our friend and lawyer, David Osnos, who traveled with us. But, within 24 hours, the intensity of the competition was so great that we all decided we needed another brain.

I suggested our brilliantly strategic friend, Sandy Greenberg. Sandy had developed a network of powerful Washingtonians from the years he worked in the White House in the 1960s, and that network had grown exponentially since. He also grew up in Buffalo and happened to know Seymour Knox III, the owner of the Buffalo Sabres hockey team, which didn't hurt. Sandy had connections and a savvy knack for working behind the scenes to make things happen. We gave him a royal greeting when he walked into our hotel room later that day.

Two new franchises were being awarded that year, but we really only had a chance for one. The son of Bill Jennings, the former chairman of the National Hockey League Board of Governors, was part of a group that was applying for a franchise in Kansas City. Because of Bill Jennings' longstanding relationship and high level of power within the National Hockey League, the assumption was that his son's group would win. That left only one franchise for many different cities to compete over.

We stayed up all night strategizing. How could we convince the Board of Governors that Washington could be a valuable asset to the league? We felt that the building and the team would be a boon to the nation's capital, but the hockey people saw Washington as a southern city with no interest in ice hockey.

We produced a host of telegrams from senators and representatives to the National Hockey League on our behalf. *"Your action would provide major league hockey and basketball for this sports-starved community and also insure a beautiful facility in the National Capital area to celebrate the Nation's bicentennial"* one telegram signed by 42 members of Congress read.

"We as members of the United States Senate join in urging you to grant a hockey franchise to the national capital area comprised of Washington, D.C. and large segments of Maryland and Virginia. One of the nation's largest urban areas is anxiously awaiting word of your decision" was another signed by 15 senators.

When Sandy Greenberg arrived, I was in my nightgown and robe, still typing letters to anyone who might give us an endorsement.

Abe personally visited all sixteen voting representatives from the sixteen NHL teams. Our plan was to sell the NHL governors on what a plus it would be to have a team in the nation's capital, playing in a brand-new arena, which already had a basketball team. If you only had one team, it would be extremely difficult to get financing for a new arena. If you had both, your chances went up significantly. We needed two teams.

For the next three days and nights, Abe would go back and forth from one room to another, visiting as many of the owners as he could. Then, exhausted, he would report back to us for our next suggestions. The biggest overall argument against our getting the team was that Washington at the time was a backwater city when it came to hockey—a southern town where no one played hockey and therefore no one would be interested in watching professionals play the sport. The NHL owners did not want a weak link. An unpopular franchise in a disinterested city would be bad for everyone's revenues.

We countered that Washington was also an international town, with embassies and embassy staffs from many countries where hockey was extremely popular. It also had many people working in government from all parts of the country. Additionally, it would bring in all kinds of entertainment—boxing matches, tennis matches, rock concerts, ice shows—all of which had bypassed Washington because the region still lacked a big enough place to perform. Then we would push Abe out the door again, and I would go back to writing letters to solicit additional support from the White House and diplomats. In that time when Abe visited the sixteen hockey team owners, none of us slept. We kept listening, discussing, and pushing Abe back out the door. Our other arguments included that the Washington metropolitan area was fast growing in population, it was an area both sports-conscious and sports-starved, and there was glamour in having a hockey team in the nation's capital! If they needed more proof of our qualifications, we were the only owners in either the NBA or the NHL who were in the construction business. Surely someone like Abe, who had just four years earlier managed to build the Irene—a huge apartment complex with 535 units and two swimming pools, a putting green, a paddleboard court with a basketball backboard, and a tennis court on the roof—would have no trouble building an arena.

There were different strategies for each governor. Aside from one moment when things did not look good and I was terrified Abe was going to have a heart attack, it was a very exciting three days and three nights.

In the end, Jack Kent Cooke, who then owned the Los Angeles Kings hockey team and was a powerful arm twister, supported us wholeheartedly. We got the franchise. Several days earlier when we arrived in Montreal, Jimmy the Greek had proclaimed the odds against our getting a hockey team at 600-1. Nothing delighted my competitive husband more than beating both those odds and Jimmy the Greek!

Now all we had to do was build the building, and as quickly as possible. Abe had read an article about a roof made of fabric that greatly shortened construction time. He contacted the architect who designed it, decided Capital Centre was going to have a fabric roof and turned the details over to Jim Clark, who was the construction manager. Jim Clark's birthday was within a day or so of Abe's birthday. "What do you say we get this done by then?" Abe asked Jim. "And then we can celebrate our birthdays together."

Capital Centre opened exactly fifteen months later, the day before Abe's birthday.

It was exciting to watch it grow. I have many pictures of the two of us at the site at various stages during the construction process—standing on the bare concrete steps, for example, before they put in the seats. There was a lot of rushing-to-finish at the end. Abe was up all night before the scheduled opening, and came home just before the festivities in need of a shower and change of clothes. It wasn't until about 4 p.m. that day that he'd gotten the necessary sewage permit to allow occupancy.

On December 2, 1973, Capital Centre opened, and the Bullets celebrated the long-awaited event by defeating the

Seattle Supersonics, 98-96, before a capacity crowd. Elvin Hayes miraculously managed to block three different shots in the last six seconds of the game.

Four days later, The Who gave a concert in the Centre. Then the Harlem Globetrotters came, then Johnny Cash, then Disney on Parade. Capital Centre brought to the Washington area something it had never had—an entertainment arena big enough for crowds of close to 20,000. Booking agents for rock bands, crooners, Ice Capades, and other kinds of entertainment took notice.

The end product was not only put together with speed, it was truly cutting edge for its time. It had a very unusual dome-shaped fabric roof, luxurious one-of-a-kind "sky suites," and featured both a giant video board and electronic ticketing, neither of which had been used in any other arena at that time.

Of course, there were some gaffes. The sky suite went unused— at least by Abe—who didn't want to watch a game that far away from the action. He insisted we sit lower, closer. And although the electronic ticketing was a remarkable time-saving device, it was not foolproof. We found out firsthand one time when we were sitting comfortably in our seats, only to be tapped on the shoulders by people holding tickets for the same seats!

Our new Capitals hockey team set a record during its first season, but not exactly the record we'd hoped for. We won eight, lost sixty-seven and tied five—far and away the worst record in the league and establishing such a low winning percentage that it remains the worst in NHL history. Coach Jim Anderson said he'd rather find out his wife was cheating on him than keep losing so badly. "At least I could tell my wife to cut it out!"

The good news was there was nowhere to go but up!

For Abe, building Capital Centre was a life-changing event. What had started as a needed distraction a decade earlier with the purchase of the Bullets was now a full-time job. The man who had never had a secretary now had several. Instead of being team owner, he was now CEO of Capital Centre, ably assisted by Jerry Sachs, his chief operating officer, and a staff of between three and four hundred people—the "Capital Centre Family." This consisted of community relations personnel, team staffs, coaches, players, trainers, ushers, and a huge operations crew capable of transforming the place from an ice hockey floor to a basketball court to a concert stage in record time. We were now in the big time.

For me, it was a continuation of the practice I had by now perfected of leading two very different lives—a day life and a night life. During the day, I was the mother of two, a member of the Board of Directors of American University, and about to become a candidate for a Master's Degree in Social Work at Catholic University. At night, I was hosting celebrities, including presidents and their entourages.

CHAPTER THREE

It wasn't always easy to separate the day from the night life, the me from the us. In 1973, at my first meeting as a member of the Board of Directors of American University, Tony Morella, the general counsel, came up to me. He began to ask questions about Abe. I stopped him.

"Tony, if you want Abe on this board, call Abe," I said. "But you have me. You decide who you want to speak to."

That wasn't the last time the issue came up for me, but it was the last time it came up with Tony, probably because there were more gripping problems for the board to deal with. Maybe he understood I intended to be a serious board member.

American University was in dire straits financially. I got a letter after joining the board from William Ahlstrom, the vice president for development and university relations. He said the school was dramatically underfunded and was struggling to survive. He doubted that American University would still exist in 1980. He left the university soon after. I wondered if I had made the right decision to join this board.

I was particularly surprised at the state of the school's library.

It was one-third as extensive as it should have been for a school its size. The university had grown very quickly in the 1960s, but the money that had been raised then was used to build dorms, not libraries. Without a first-rate library, the school would never grow and never be equal to other local schools.

The major topic of discussion of the board became how to build a new library. We recognized that we had to do something about this, but what and how?

As a new board member and with my love for books and libraries, I wanted to be a part of this project. I felt that I could bring in new energy and new contacts.

I had just begun working at the Neurology Center in Chevy Chase. I didn't have my own office and was working at one of the doctor's desks. I made my first list of contacts. I remembered that some of our builder friends were American University graduates, and called them. Surely they would want to support their old school, but I was totally taken aback. Several had no interest in supporting the school or being identified with it. I was counting on that support. Where would I go?

I suggested to the president that we hire a "development professional." Once he was onboard, I worked very closely with him. He brought me lists of some of the wealthy people in Washington, some of whom I had heard of or knew slightly, but none had had any previous connection to the school. Why did he think they would give money to American University?

Even though I was not a professional fund-raiser, I understood why someone would not want to support just any cause. I was embarrassed to be telling him something I felt he should have known.

"Just because they have money doesn't mean they're going to give it to you," I told him. "You have to approach them with something that interests them, something they care about."

One day at my desk, I remember squeezing my brain for ideas.

What could we (the university) offer someone as an opportunity to be involved in something they cared about? What do some of our friends care about that they would support, no matter where?

Because we were in the building business, I knew a lot of Jewish Washington businessmen socially. I knew what they cared about—Jewish studies, Jewish history, Jewish culture. Why not establish a special section in the new American University Library called the "National Center for American Judaism" and give it a prominent place in the new building?

The board and the university staff agreed to try my plan, and I began making phone calls. For one day, I made ten phone calls and I got ten contributors to give $10,000 each, $100,000. The idea of creating a center to study Judaism—the first in Washington—was very appealing.

It was also the spark needed to fund the library. We next solicited 100 corporations to contribute to a business and industry section of the new library. Two years later, the new American University Library opened. It was three times the size of the old library with twice as many volumes. I was very proud of the accomplishment and am still to this day; proud not only of the library, but of the school as a whole. American University is now a prestigious university and the Jewish Studies Center has grown and thrived. There is no plaque at the library with my name on it, but I know the part I played in pulling American University out of the depths. It proved to me what I could do on my own. I was very pleased with myself. This was Irene Pollin.

===============

Another one of the major and best decisions I ever made on my own was to go to Catholic University's School of Social Work. I loved my three years at Catholic. The training, knowledge, and experience I received provided skills that have served me ever since, for my work as well as my personal life.

It opened my eyes to a new world and taught me so much about people, personalities, and relationships—as well as how to think—all of which have become central to my way of doing things. It completely changed the way I think about everything.

As I was completing my third and final year at Catholic, I knew I had to write a master's thesis, but on what? I kept putting off the decision. Then, one evening, while attending a class on death and dying I had an epiphany. At one point, the professor asked members of the class to recount any personal experiences they had had with death and dying.

It was a small class, about eight students, all of whom were younger than I. We were sitting in a semicircle and could see each other's faces. As each student spoke of some personal experience with death, I sat wondering what I would do when it came to me.

Listening to each of their stories, I realized that I was the only one in the class who had lost people who were very close to me. Most of them talked about the death of some distant relative or friend. *"I'll never forget how I felt when I heard that my uncle in California was dying of cancer."*

I was sitting there, frozen in my chair. I was still feeling the loss of my sixteen-year-old daughter almost ten years earlier. What could I say to these people? As it came closer to my turn to speak, I struggled with whether or not to relate my experience with Linda. Then I would have to tell them about Jay Jay, too.

Up to then, I had not been willing to open up about my loss to hardly anyone, much less a group of strangers. My heart was pounding so loudly, I could barely hear myself think, but my mind was pushing me. *It may help you! Say something. You have to. It will help them! It will shock them! This is a chance to tell your story.*

I began shaking involuntarily, but I made up my mind I would do it. Would I break down? I just blurted it out. "I lost two children," I said. "My fifteen-month-old infant son and my sixteen-year-old daughter."

There was a dead silence in the room, a terrible silence. Luckily for me, there was no discussion after that because it was time for a coffee break. As I walked out of the room, I was relieved. I didn't have to elaborate. I couldn't believe that I had actually said those words out loud. It was a breakthrough. I was still shaking as we walked out in the hall to the counter where we put our coffee cups. A nun in the class who I had befriended joined me. In earlier classes, we had commiserated about how difficult it was to think of a thesis topic. But this time she said, "Irene, I think you have your topic. You should write about your experience with the death of your daughter and son. It would help so many people."

She changed my life and I don't even remember her name.

In the days that followed, I thought a lot about what she said, especially the part about being able to "help so many people." The idea of making something positive out of my tragedy was very appealing. This might be a way for me to finally come to terms with my tragedy, since I was still taking medication to help me cope. I decided the title of my thesis would be "A Dying Adolescent." Believe it or not, even as I chose the title, I still wasn't connecting me to the subject. I thought, *this is a good research topic. I know a lot about it.* But it was not going to be about my daughter. It was still too close for comfort. This was ten years after my daughter died, and I still couldn't deal with the issue. The pain was still too close.

I wrote the thesis as a detached social worker, not a mother. I was a theorist explaining how the adolescent looked at death and its effect on the family. The adolescent wasn't Linda. I was not ready to go there.

While I was researching my topic, I went to the National Library of Medicine in Bethesda to see what had been written on the subject. There were exactly two books, and both were terrible. *Was this all the information there was about death and dying? And how about living with the illness before you die? Surely there was more about living and coping with an illness.*

This was when Elisabeth Kübler-Ross came out with her book, *On Death and Dying.* I had heard her speak at a conference at Children's Hospital in Washington, and was so impressed with her theory that I contacted her. What impressed me was that she recognized the need for someone to speak openly about death and dying and not to keep it secret, quiet, inside. This resonated with me; my need to know more, to do more, to be able to speak about my losses rather than keeping the pain inside my body.

However, I also recognized that she had not worked with any of the patients she presented; she had only visited them briefly in a hospital setting. This was quite different from working with them and their families over a lengthy period of time. But she had come up with an interesting theory, and the idea of being open about death and dying was new and appealing. For too long people had felt uncomfortable about discussing it.

I joined a small group of theologians and therapists who were very interested in this new theory about death and dying. We all felt strongly there needed to be more information about something everyone would eventually deal with. There was none available even for trained counselors. We had been getting together regularly for quite a while when I had a strange experience at one meeting held in a church. There were only six of us sitting in the large sanctuary. On my way in, I saw a casket in the lobby. As I walked down the aisle to join my colleagues, I had a powerful feeling in my gut. I knew then that I did not want to talk about death and caskets; I wanted to talk about life and living. I was interested in *living* with, not *dying* from, a terminal illness. That evening changed the direction of my work and my relationship with the group. I needed to go in a different direction.

In the work I had done with dying patients, I had observed that people who were dying were not preoccupied with dying; they were occupied with living until the moment they died.

They may have known that they had not long to live, but they were still *living*.

=============

One summer morning in 1974, I was at home, working on my graduate thesis, when I received a call from a friend. He asked if Abe and I might be interested in taking over a house on the beach in Rehoboth, Delaware that he had rented for the summer. He was recovering from a ski accident and was unable to get there.

At the time, Abe's older brother Jack had been quite ill with cancer and I knew he loved the beach. I suggested to Abe that perhaps we could share the season; Jack could sit on the wonderful deck facing the ocean and recuperate. Abe loved the beach. It was an easy sell.

It was a bright and cheerful semi-detached house. The best part was being able to walk three steps from the deck onto the sand and another 30 feet to the Atlantic Ocean. Unfortunately, Jack never got there. But Abe and I did and loved it. I was able to complete my thesis. As we were leaving the beach for home, I noticed the house two doors down was for sale. I suddenly had an idea. "Honey, let's buy this house," I told Abe. "We can use it as a getaway on weekends as well as the summer. It's only two-and-a-half hours from Capital Centre. We can drive straight there on a Friday night after a game." He picked up on the idea and we drove home talking about how wonderful it could be for us and Robert and his family who were now living California. As was typical, Abe did not want to miss an opportunity. The minute we walked in to our house, he was on the phone, calling the owner. We bought the beach house in ten minutes, sight unseen, over the phone.

A few weeks later, we spent our first night there. The previous owners had left all their furniture, which was fine with us for the time being. We were just so happy to actually have a house at the beach. Lying there in my peacock-blue bed I was happy as a lark, fully appreciating that I was in my wonderful new beach house. In the darkness, with the sound of the ocean outside of my window, I imagined all the great times we were going to have. Then, as I stretched out, my hand reached behind into the slat in the headboard and I felt something bite my finger. In the dark, I yelled, "Oh, my God, it's a mouse!" "Honey, it's a mouse!" I heard him scamper away.

"What do you want me to do about it?" Abe said, half asleep.

Standing on top of my bed, I yelled, "Go get him!"

Stumbling in the dark, Abe ran downstairs, found an old broom, and began chasing the poor, frightened animal around our bedroom. Until he assured me he had chased the mouse out of the house, I would not come off the top of the bed.

I soon learned that the house wouldn't take care of itself.

===============

After I graduated from Catholic University in 1974, I got a job at Children's Hospital in Washington in the Department of Psychiatry.

I was assigned to the dialysis, burn, and emergency room units. These were extremely difficult assignments and I knew that, but I wanted the challenge; I wanted to test what I could and could not handle. I loved my work there. I had the opportunity to not only work with families who were dealing with long-term illnesses, but also with outstanding doctors. One was Dr. Reginald Lourie, a world-renowned child psychiatrist. He became my mentor.

I discovered that, like me a decade earlier, people who were dealing with chronic illness and death—either their own or that of a family member—were still not getting any meaningful help.

Working with these patients and families, I began to think these people didn't need to go to a psychiatrist. I knew that from my own experience. Recommending a psychiatrist amounts to telling a patient dealing with a serious illness that he or she has yet another illness, a mental one, and that's not true. He or she simply needs help dealing with the physical illness. Yes, these are emotional issues, but they are caused by the physical illness. The same is true for family members. They are dealing with a deeply distressing medical situation. The challenge for them is how to get through it, move on with their lives, and not destroy their relationships in the process.

It was then I decided I was going to specialize in helping people cope with the problems created by a long-term or life-threatening medical problem. A few years later, as my own private practice was expanding, I came up with the name, "Medical Crisis Counseling"— "counseling" instead of "therapy," because I thought it would be easier to accept counseling around a medical problem than therapy around a psychiatric problem. My thesis would be: You're not clinically depressed; you were diagnosed with a medical illness. How could you not be sad? It is only normal to be depressed in this situation. However, there are ways of coping, ways of learning to live with the situation. And that's where I felt that I could help people. In 1975, I set up a small office in Chevy Chase to help patients and their families cope with long-term illness. How does one manage on a day-to-day basis? What kinds of adjustments do patients and the families need to make, and what help do they need in making them? What can be done to enhance the experience of living for patients who know they are dying?

As I worked on my master's thesis, I had found that hardly any research had been done on these issues. I knew from the very beginning I would be covering new ground. I was completely taken with the idea of helping normal people cope with the abnormal circumstance of being diagnosed with a chronic illness.

I wrote to several local doctors explaining what I was interested in doing and asking them to refer patients to me. I heard from several, but realized at that time there was a huge gap between what medical doctors thought they needed to do for their patients and what I was proposing. They were trained to deal with bodies, not emotions, and most were perfectly comfortable keeping things that way. Their goal was to administer the best physical treatment possible. Recognizing the importance of dealing with problems that might be linked to the illness and treating those problems were something else.

Fortunately for me, Dr. Marvin Korengold, a neurologist who operated the Neurology Center in Chevy Chase, Maryland, was way ahead of his time. He saw that the kind of counseling I was doing could be of value to his patients, since neurological diseases by and large are chronic and incurable, diseases you have to learn to live with. Dr. Korengold invited me to join his practice and, understanding full well what an incredible opportunity this would be for me, I jumped at his offer, gave up my new office and moved into a suite of offices he set up for me on another floor in his building.

Within hours of my settling in with my new staplers, tape, pencils, and paper, Dr. Korengold walked into my office with my first patient, a young woman. He had just given her a diagnosis of multiple sclerosis, and she was in shock. This was exactly what I wanted, but I was in over my head.

Francine was single, in her twenties and as she sat down in front of me, her eyes filled with tears.

"I just got a promotion at work this week," she told me, her voice choking, "I was so proud. And now suddenly…everything is over. My life is over. I just moved to Washington last year. Now, I'm going home."

I was caught off guard. Her blow was so sudden, and I was not prepared. What could I say to her that would help her deal with this traumatic blow? I tried to bring her back to the present—to the fact that, at the moment, her health was not so different from what it had been earlier in the week, and that MS was often a slow-moving disease. She should take time to digest the news.

However, she barely heard what I had said to her. I spent several hours hoping to calm her down, help her organize her thinking. But, as I learned later on, she indeed left the city. Her immediate reaction was to run, leave town, leave her job and her friends. She wanted to go home. Even though I tried to convince her not to make any quick decisions, her instincts took over. Perhaps that was the best decision at the time. She needed time to integrate what the doctor had told her just a few hours earlier.

It is important to see patients fairly soon after their diagnosis, because it is in the early stage—the crisis stage—that people were most open to therapy. But there was such a thing as too soon. This was the lesson I took away as a new therapist from the experience with Francine. This young woman had had no more than five minutes from the time she was told she had multiple sclerosis to the time I saw her! And, even though I spent several hours with her, she needed to be hugged by people who loved her.

===============

I didn't have much time to dwell on my mistakes that evening because President Carter was coming to a basketball game. The Bullets were hosting the Atlanta Hawks—the Georgia-based team—and he, his wife, Rosalynn, and daughter, Amy, were joining us at the game.

"The President will sit here," the Secret Service told us.

Unfortunately "here" was where Abe always sat and Abe was not one to relinquish turf. "No way," Abe told the Secret Service. "That's my seat."

"But, sir, we're talking about the President of the United States."

"He can have any seat in the building," Abe told them. "But this is my seat."

Abe won the argument. President Carter sat next to Abe in my usual seat and I sat on the other side of him.

"This might be a bit awkward," Abe warned the President, knowing that he would be rooting for his home team.

"Won't be," President Carter assured him. "I am, after all, President of the whole United States!" He smiled. "I'm not going to root for Atlanta."

That may have been his plan, but it turned out to be easier said than done. Once the game started, he couldn't contain himself. He began yelling as loudly as he could to the Atlanta team—"Get the ball!" "Yes!"

Abe and Irene Pollin, owners of the Bullets, diplomatically suggested that it might be better if he sat in a different seat!

We agreed and he moved to the other side of me.

The Bullets ended up winning, but it was a very close game. Toward the end, when the Secret Service suggested that he should leave to avoid the mob scene that always occurred when a game ended, President Carter complied. But he walked very slowly. We laughed as we spied him standing behind the basket watching intently to the bitter end, hoping for a miracle.

Stephanie was younger than the first patient I saw with a new diagnosis. She'd had a full month to digest her MS diagnosis.

"I'm damaged goods," she told me. "I belong in a bargain basement." She felt her entire life had been turned upside down, but it was Stephanie's more immediate concerns that brought her to me. She feared she didn't have the physical strength or the concentration necessary to get through the bar exam she'd been preparing for the past three years.

Her overall problem was coping with the MS diagnosis, but now she had to find a way to pass her bar exam. The stakes here were high—failing would not only make her feel all those years of law school and the weeks of cramming for the bar were lost, it would also be the first serious loss caused by her illness. Together, we decided to concentrate on getting through the bar exam. After she passed, we would deal with the MS.

We went over breathing tips for relaxing during the exam and then considered the practical details together. Where would the exam be held? What was the room like? Would there be breaks? Where could she relax during the break? Could she bring food or drink into the room? Each of the questions seemed to bring out ways Stephanie could handle the situation. The more questions she answered in my office, the less anxious she became about the forthcoming exam.

The next week she took the exam and passed. This was the first time since Stephanie found out she had multiple sclerosis that she had experienced a sense of control over her life.

She was jubilant. Once again, I had learned something. Stephanie had been overwhelmed by the enormity of the challenges she knew lay ahead, but by planning specific, achievable goals she had been able to distinguish present fears from future ones, real problems from fear-generated ones. She was one of my success stories. I was thrilled to be able to make a difference in her young life.

I was also very fortunate that a wonderful woman, Margaret Patton, was working for Dr. Korengold at the time. She had been his first office manager, watching his practice grow from one doctor to nine and a large staff. Over time, her job had evolved into talking to patients on the phone whenever they were depressed and frustrated with their worsening conditions. She understood completely what I planned to do and offered to work with me. This was an additional blessing. She knew all the patients in the practice.

She also understood my goal—to enable these people with incurable chronic illnesses to go on living as well as possible, to live their lives as fully as they could. She also understood there was virtually no research on this new goal of mine. This presented a wonderful opportunity to learn and practice.

With her, I decided to begin a group of young, female MS patients, average age 25—an age I felt that I could have the most impact on their futures. Within two weeks, I began interviewing many young women. My goal was to learn the major issues in their lives that were affected by the MS diagnosis. I interviewed for several months, narrowing down to ten women who would be good candidates for my first group. These issues, learned from those first interviews, became the central theme of my future work with chronically ill patients and their families and eventually the subject of my book, *Medical Crisis Counseling*.

Listening to each one, I searched for basic truths, ones that applied to anyone coping with a chronic illness. One of the first insights I had was that the primary issue was the physical illness; any emotional, psychological responses were due to the disease. Yes, they were all dealing with depression, fear, and anger, but wouldn't that be a normal response to the change in their lives, in their physical condition?

They weren't crazy, no matter how overwhelmed they felt emotionally. They weren't having breakdowns. They were facing a major life change, one that they had to adjust to no matter how they might deny it.

If I could help them understand they were supposed to feel this way, it would help them adjust and eventually accept their situation; given the circumstances, their feelings were normal. It also allowed them to feel free to express any feelings they had been suppressing or denying.

I did a lot of listening during the initial group sessions and, as a result, a lot of learning. I listened to which issues seemed to surface earlier and which later. And every patient dealt with all of them in much the same order, but to a different degree depending on the individual personality and personal situation. Once these issues came to the surface, the patients were able to face them and get beyond them. I was amazed at how consistently those issues appeared in those first sessions and throughout my years of practice. I also built the number of sessions for each patient on the eight issues, plus the consult and final session; this became my ten-session model. It was to be a short-term contract. The idea was not to add another "illness" or "treatment" for someone dealing with a lifelong illness. This was also a treatment with a foreseeable end.

The eight issues are: control, self-image, dependency, stigma, abandonment, anger, isolation, and death. Stephanie exhibited the first two: the fear of losing control and a much-changed self-image. Her fear of not being able to complete her bar exam, and then her description of herself as "damaged goods." The other issues surfaced as well, but wanting to get her through her upcoming deadline, we concentrated on these two.

The others eventually followed. For example, the dependency on her family, the way people looked differently at her now at work (stigma), the fear of being abandoned by friends, the anger at the situation, the feeling of being isolated from others, and finally, the fear of dying.

As I learned over my many years of practice, each patient often dealt with one dominant issue.

For Sam, who was diagnosed with MS in his twenties, people's perceptions of him dominated his thinking. For many years, he appeared to be perfectly normal until he began having trouble walking. Wanting to hide it ultimately became a problem, particularly for his wife. His wife needed him to get a wheelchair, but he fought her until one day she came in crying. She felt she could no longer bear the burden of managing his walking, and additionally, keeping it secret.

Fortunately, he loved and respected her. When I saw him privately and explained how she felt, he yielded. She had not been able to tell him how she felt either. Within a few weeks, Sam and his wife reported he was racing his sons in his new wheelchair.

Members of a patient's family often deal with the same set of issues as the patient. They encounter challenges to their ability to control their own lives while caring for a sick relative. They deal with the dependency of the sick person on them, the stigma of feeling embarrassed about the condition of a sick relative, and the guilt about feeling that way. They have to process grief and loss too, and understand the negative emotions like anger that the illness arouses. Because of this, and the importance of their mental strength on the patient's quality of life, I worked with many family members, particularly spouses, in separate sessions.

I also worked to get both the patient and the family members to understand each other's issues. When you're totally hung up on your own misery, being forced to see the other side takes you out of yourself. This not only helps the relationship, but also helps the patient know that he is not alone in coping with his situation—a powerful antidote to depression.

=============

Sometimes it was hard to reconcile my daytime and my evening activities. During the day, I quietly sat in my chair facing each patient, one on one, as a non threatening therapist, using the language of the medical and psychiatric worlds.

My night was the total opposite from the minute I stepped into the noisy, throbbing, lights-flashing building that was Capital Centre. I usually sat next to Abe watching our teams win and lose, and then deal occasionally with the celebrities who came to perform. Ordinarily, we did not meet and greet them, but some— like Frank Sinatra—demanded more attention than the President.

The first time Frank Sinatra came to perform in our building, he insisted that Abe and I meet him officially before the concert and be there when his limousine pulled up to the entrance to welcome him amidst press fanfare, with photographer flash bulbs going off.

The problem was that the arena was circular and there were four different, equal entrances. Each time we approached a designated entrance his car was at another one. The result became a circus. We kept going round and round on the inside of the building as his limo went round and round on the outside. We wondered what was causing the problem, and discovered that every time he approached an entrance and there weren't enough reporters, he would tell the driver to go to the next one. Finally, Abe and I had had it. We were about to give up when Sinatra finally found an entrance he liked and got out of the car. We were not too warm and kissy at that point.

Abe loved to tell the story of having Muhammad Ali in his office. "How would you like to be the most famous, the most powerful person in the world? I can lick anyone in the whole world!" He was a total charmer.

Life at Capital Centre was constantly eventful. "Sometimes it should be boring," I'd say to Abe, but we never had boring. In addition to dealing with celebrities and booking agents, there was also the challenge of negotiating with the people who represented them. Irvin Feld's Barnum and Bailey Circus was a case in point. Feld was a brilliant businessman, a very tough guy, and every issue—whether it had to do with rent, concessions, expenses— had to be done his way or no way. He knew he had a unique product, and the arenas needed and wanted his show.

But Abe was not a man who liked doing things someone *else's* way. At one point, he got so fed up with Feld, he decided he didn't need Barnum and Bailey; he would create his own circus. It took six months to hire all the people. And, in 1974, Circus America performed before a huge crowd at Capital Centre. Abe even got to ride on one of the elephants. After two seasons, Abe decided this was not for him, but I loved the fact that he tried.

Washington was beginning to become a major city for top entertainment. There had never before been an arena in the nation's capital large enough or sophisticated enough to accommodate these groups that were appearing in every other large city. Mike Crowley, general manager of Capital Centre, was always looking for new events. In 1974, he suggested that we go to Russia to look at a musical ice show in Kiev.

He didn't know how much Abe and I enjoyed unusual experiences, and it didn't take much coaxing to get us to go. While in Russia, Abe could try to get some Russian hockey players for our team. They were the best players in the world.

And so we went. The show was in Kiev, but we went to Moscow first.

Moscow, in the early 1970s, was not very elegant. We were put up in the best hotel suite, crystal chandeliers, and rich Persian carpets, but the toilet tank was on the ceiling. We knew we were being treated royally, communist-style. But we weren't looking at the quality of the furnishings; we were just thrilled to be there. The anticipation of meeting with the heads of the Russian Hockey League was so exciting we could barely sleep. Abe and I talked all night, planning what he would say to convince them to send some of their players to our team.

The morning after we arrived, at exactly 8 a.m., a knock on the door announced the arrival of the gentleman who would take Abe to his first meeting. I was to wait in the suite until he returned, which I presumed would not take very long. However, several hours later, there was another knock on the door. This time it was Abe. Jubilant, almost hyper, he couldn't wait to tell me what occurred. I could barely sit still while he related the details of his first meeting.

Abe and Mike Crowley attended the meeting with the two heads of the Russian Hockey League. They had a translator and decided to meet again the following day. But that evening, after dinner, Abe and I combed our rooms for any possible bugs. After we searched every possible hiding place, including, of course, the crystal chandeliers, we decided that any further conversation we might have regarding Abe's strategy for the next meeting would be done in the bathroom with the shower going full blast. Knowing that they were listening, it was all we could do to keep from laughing out loud. This was so much fun! We could barely wait until the following morning for the next meeting.

Again, promptly at 8 a.m., the same courier came to take Abe to the meeting. But this time, still at the door, he told us what the meeting would consist of. How did he know what Abe had in mind?

Several hours later, Abe returned with the following details of his meeting. He had told them how impressed he was with the Russian players and what a coup it would be to have two play in the capital of the United States, Washington, D.C. He offered a million dollars for the two players, believing that was a generous offer. His Russian counterpart responded, this time without the translator and in perfect English, "But, Mr. Pollin, Bobby Orr and Phil Esposito earn more than that." In the end, they were unwilling to send any players to the U.S., regardless of the amount of money. We thought money was not the issue, but rather they were afraid the players would defect. Abe's attempt to bring two rather than one was so they would be company for each other with less chance for a defection. But, it obviously wasn't a strong enough argument.

Next we went to Kiev to see the ice show. As luck would have it, the tough Russian winter came crashing down and we were unable to travel. We sat in the hotel room until it was decided to put us on a train. Even the train was delayed, and by the time we finally made it to Kiev, we had missed the final performance.

At this time, the Soviet Union was a communist dictatorship. The powerful could do whatever they wanted. "Never mind," they told us. "You will see the show anyway." And with that they arranged to perform a complete ice show—with a full cast and an orchestra—just for Abe and me.

It was the strangest experience—two pairs of hands clapping in a huge, empty arena, an entire ice show performed for an audience of two! We knew we were being observed for our reaction. The show was quite beautiful and we enthusiastically approved for it to come to Capital Centre the following year. My husband was a big shot impresario! This was an exciting time for Abe and me.

=============

My practice at the Neurology Center was also expanding. The practice model I had envisioned was working. All of the group therapy sessions with patients were short term, designed to last only three months. The goal was to bring patients from a sense of helplessness to a sense of mastery. Short-term therapy could not alter the course of their disease, but it could help them cope, psychologically and emotionally. Helping them regain a level of control of their lives and lowering their stress level could even possibly slow the disease process.

Being able to experiment a bit, I decided to form a group with three young MS patients who appeared to have so much in common.

The three women were all in their late twenties and beautiful blonds. Each one was prettier than the next, and they were all in wheelchairs. I believed they would have so much to share with each other, and I worked for over a year to make the group happen. It took that long for several reasons. I had to convince each one how it might be beneficial, I had to find a location in my offices that was wheelchair accessible, and a room where each could sit and face each other.

One afternoon, I got them together. I was filled with hope about the possibilities of what we could accomplish. As a therapist, I was pleased that these three women had put their trust in me and they were willing to try this experiment.

It was a failure. As each of the young women wheeled themselves into the room and faced their counterparts, they were not thrilled as I had hoped; they were shocked. Their faces gave away all their feelings. I knew it was mistake. I quickly suggested that we meet separately.

What I thought would be a positive experience—meeting

someone in the same condition—was in fact, a negative. They were mirror images of each other. While each woman did not recognize in her reflection the changes the illness had brought, she could see it in the others. It was something none of them wished to confront.

I was still learning what would work and what wouldn't.

Luckily, I had built up trust with each of these women that allowed them all to continue their therapy with me.

=============

What does every professional sports team owner dream of, plan for, and do almost anything for? If you know anything about this world, you know it is to win a championship. Most teams never accomplish this, but they never give up trying. We were no different than any of the others.

From the day we bought the Bullets in 1964, Abe's promise to me was that when we won the championship, we would celebrate wildly. For fourteen years, this was the elusive goal; always sitting there in front of us, teasing us as we carefully planned those years' players, coaches, and schedules. If we get so-and-so, will he be the one who can get us there?

Getting there is a science, as I learned. It is a most complicated process—half knowledge, half guessing. And, there are the things that can happen you can't plan for, particularly player injuries. Putting the right players together who have skills that match and complement the others is one thing. But also the mental and psychological attitudes and mood of the team must blend into one cohesive, smoothly functioning group for the full schedule of games as they travel from city to city. When this happens for a team, it is actually quite rare. Some teams, once they have reached that difficult goal of a well-balanced winning team, can win one or more championships. Some teams never reach that goal.

We reached that goal in 1978. We had some injuries, but fewer serious ones, and the on-court chemistry among the players was very good. As we moved along in the season, we began to feel a sense that something big could happen. We had a great starting lineup that year—power forward Elvin Hayes, who had a turnaround, fade-away jumper that was almost impossible to block; legendary rebounder Wes Unseld, who was famous for his bone-jarring picks and outlet passes and ended up being selected Most Valuable Player in the finals; smooth-shooting Bobby Dandridge, who we'd just acquired for his strong defensive moves; and high scorers Kevin Grevey and Tom Henderson.

As our team continued to win and we were moving forward, we now felt confident enough to have a mantra. When we were leading the San Antonio Spurs in the Eastern Conference semifinals, one sportscaster warned, "The opera isn't over until the fat lady sings." Our coach Dick Motta picked up the phrase and used it time and again, both to caution the team against over confidence and to inspire them to win games in which the Bullets were underdogs. The 1977-1978 season was not over until the fat lady sang for us.

She sang in game seven in Seattle. When the celebrating players ripped off Dick Motta's shirt at the end of the game, they found he was wearing one of many T-shirts he'd printed for the occasion. "The opera isn't over until the fat lady sings" was emblazoned across it, with the coach's signature underneath.

What an incredibly exciting time! It really happened! You hope. You pray. You think it's possible, but you don't think it will really happen. And then it did!

From what lofty perch did we watch this most important moment of our lives? At the Seattle Center Coliseum, Abe and I and our guests were escorted to probably the worst seats in the entire building. The usher apologized to us. He was embarrassed that his boss, SuperSonics owner Sam Schulman, had given us seats that were literally four rows down from the top of the building. As our group got to our seats, local fans sitting near us commented," You're the OWNERS of the other team and Mr. Schulman put you HERE?"

They could not believe it. Truthfully, at that point, we really didn't care. We just wanted to leave that building with a championship.

It happened. We won! There is nothing like that moment when you actually win. Now my husband, who had been promising me this co-celebration for 14 years, shot up out of his seat, jumping down the many steps from our sky-level seats and headed for the locker room, totally forgetting me. Within seconds, he was ahead of the crowd and I couldn't follow him. The crowd was blocking my way.

If I had been able to put my hands around his throat at that moment, I would have—only I first had to reach him in the locker room. These players were guys I had known and cheered for all these years. I too wanted to hug and be hugged. By the time I got through the crowd and made it to the locker room, everyone was drenched in champagne. It was exactly what one dreamed of when you win a championship. Even Abe and I hugged. There's a wonderful picture of Abe and me that someone took on the plane going home that tells the story. There are three seats. Abe is sitting at one end near the window, I'm at the other, and the trophy is in the seat between us. The expression on my face tells exactly how I felt at the time.

A big victory is a big victory. Something we had hoped could come our way some day did.

We made up pretty quickly. Everyone was so high from our experience. We almost didn't need the plane to get us home. As we were approaching the airport in the large charter plane, the pilot said to Abe, "They estimate there are about 10,000 people down there. Do you want me to bypass this and go into another airport? If I land here, you're going to find yourself in the middle of a mob scene."

"Are you crazy?" Abe answered, "We waited fourteen years to get to this mob scene. Get us down there!"

Oh, the euphoria! As the pilot predicted, we were mobbed, and we loved every second of it. Then we all piled into open cars taking us down a parade route on Pennsylvania Avenue, and then to a reception at the White House with President Carter.

Next was a ceremony in the District Building again attended by screaming crowds. This was a rather frightening moment for me. Sitting on the stage, I was sitting beside the team during the ceremonies and speeches. When it was over, everyone rushed to get to the players. As the crowd pushed forward, I found myself getting pushed back. And, even though I called and reached for some of the players, the noise was so great that they couldn't hear me. As I was about to be crushed against the back brick wall of the stage, someone lifted me up—straight up in the air—and stood me on top of one of the chairs. Wes Unseld saved my life. Another few minutes and I would have been crushed. Abe loved Wes, not just because he was a great player. I love Wes also but not just because he was a great player. He is an extraordinary human being.

Our team was known worldwide, and extraordinary opportunities were open to us. We were invited to play abroad in places where NBA teams had never visited. Abe liked being the first of whatever, so soon he was making arrangements for these trips and included players' wives and girlfriends.

We first traveled to Israel, where they love basketball—the first NBA team to make the trip. The plan was for the players to visit many important places: Jerusalem, the Galilee, Tiberius, a kibbutz, the Dead Sea, and the ruins at Masada.

But the centerpiece of the trip was a game between the Bullets and the Israeli Maccabees. The world champion Bullets lost 98-97. Rather amazing considering the professional experience of both teams, but a good deal of referee cheating, calling fouls that weren't fouls, helped.

We had to laugh because what they were doing was rather obvious, but the players took it in stride. These were sophisticated guys; they knew what was happening and found it amusing. They had come to Israel for a vacation and were enjoying themselves. If the Israelis really wanted to win the game that badly, well, let them have it.

One person who took the game very seriously was Ruth, the ex-wife of Israeli Foreign Minister Moshe Dayan.

At the game, she sat in the row in front of Leah Rabin and me. When we went to the ladies' room at half time, she berated Leah in Hebrew as loudly as she could. "You're rooting for the other team! How could you!" But, Leah was our friend as well as our guest, so that's how!

The next day, everyone in Israel talked about the game they had won from the American champions. They still talk about it. At the U.S. Embassy that night, the ambassador acknowledged what had really happened and admitted the result was good for Israeli morale. We still laugh about it.

A year later, in 1979, President Jimmy Carter normalized relations with China. Abe decided to try for another first: Be the first U.S. professional sports team to visit China. The U.S. had sent just about every amateur sports team over there—diving, basketball, soccer, volleyball, and of course, ping-pong. But, we would be the first professional sports team.

He talked to people at the State Department, who talked to the Chinese. The next thing we knew, we got an official invitation from China. We were thrilled at the prospect. Abe and I had been to Hong Kong, but never to China. What an incredible opportunity and, again, we would be taking not only the players, but their wives and girlfriends as well.

China in 1979 was very different from China today. Mao Zedong had died three years earlier and the country was emerging from a long period of isolation. We could barely contain the excitement of what we envisioned we'd experience.

After a very long flight, we landed at night in Beijing—the capital of the country—and we were one of only three airplanes in the entire dark airport. Soon, two buses pulled up, an old, rickety school bus and a more modern minibus. Used to being treated deferentially, the players began climbing into the minibus only to be told by Chinese authorities that it was reserved for the team executives. My immediate reaction was: *Since when do communists give special privileges to the capitalist owners?*

Like the airport, the roads to the city were dark and empty, not a car in sight and few streetlights. Driving into the city, we saw children sitting in the middle of the road under these sparsely placed lights playing cards. They didn't expect any speeding cars to interrupt their game.

Another Washingtonian also happened to be in town on an official visit: Vice President Walter Mondale. I was happy he was there to improve relations, but his party was taking up valuable and precious space in the best hotel in Beijing. We were relegated to a room without air-conditioning. Our "suite" consisted of two iron bed frames with sagging mattresses, an ancient bathroom with broken tiles, and bugs in the dresser drawers. The players found the hotel beds so small they ended up putting their mattresses on the floor. When we woke up the next morning and looked out the window, we saw wall-to-wall bicycles—thousands of people in Mao uniforms passing by on bicycles in a remarkably orderly fashion. Not one car.

The Chinese love basketball. Wherever we saw empty space in a city, be it Beijing or Shanghai or Canton, where we traveled later, we'd see a basketball hoop. When our coach Dick Motta held a "coaches clinic" with some of the players, 7,000 coaches came from all over the country to attend.

At that time, the Chinese had not seen many foreigners in their country. Our huge black and white basketball players were definitely standouts. So was their athletic gear. Adidas and Puma shoes had not yet made it to China. Wherever the players went, they were surrounded by crowds. When the players brought out their Polaroid cameras, which were extremely popular in the U.S., the people went wild. The players had a wonderful time; taking pictures, giving them away to mobs in Tiananmen Square. Hundreds of people surrounded the players, and the crowd lifted up one person and passed him forward. It turned out he could speak English, and the Chinese wanted him to translate as they asked the players questions. They were a very friendly crowd and extremely curious.

When Wes Unseld decided to go for a run one morning, he kept going straight so he could turn around and retrace his steps back to the hotel. The sight of a tall black man running down the street in shorts was so unusual that some Chinese people began to run with him. The group of joggers became so large that Wes got distracted. He got totally lost and surrounded by people who could only offer directions in Chinese. He was having visions of roaming the streets of Beijing for the rest of his life when he spotted one of the camera crews which had come to China with the team.

There weren't many tourists in China. Nothing underscored that more than the fact that when we went to the Great Wall with the players, the only other tourists we bumped into were Walter Mondale and Sargent Shriver, fellow Washingtonians. We were so glad to see each other that we quickly took pictures of each other.

Our group was completely overwhelmed by the size and scale of the Great Wall. How could this have been built? And why? To everyone's surprise, there was one person who had absolutely no interest.

All of us—the players and wives—hopped excitedly off the bus, but Elvin Hayes sat still.

"Aren't you coming with us?" Abe asked.

Elvin shrugged. "I've seen big walls before."

"Not like this," Wes Unseld added. "This wall is the only man-made structure that can be seen from outer space!"

Elvin stared him down. "I'm never going into outer space."

"One of the wonders of the world," Abe angrily whispered to me, "and he didn't even get off the bus."

The Chinese arranged all of our tour. And as we began to move around the city, we got the impression we were free to go wherever, but sensed we were being monitored.

The day before we were to play an evening game against the Chinese Army team in Beijing, we were taken for a casual walk in a park. The terrain was quite rough. We were climbing up and down, up and down. Even though we were young and strong, it was difficult walking. It was several hours before I realized what was happening. "They're trying to wear the players out before the game!" This was not an unknown phenomenon in the NBA. We cut the park tour short.

The Chinese played by international rules and we played by American rules, so a decision had to be made before the game on which rules we'd follow. Abe, Jerry Sachs, and I were sitting in a visitor's room drinking tea and negotiating—working through a translator—as a crowd of 19,000 outside was screaming for the game to begin. Abe was a great negotiator, but the Chinese were intractable. "I have the solution," the Chinese negotiator announced. "For the first half of the game we'll play by Chinese rules, and then we'll see after that!"

The Chinese had found a giant to play opposite Wes Unseld. Their center's name was Mu and he was 7 foot 3 inches and weighed more than 300 pounds. Described by our General Manager Bob Ferry as "the biggest pagoda we've seen in China," Mu— fortunately for us—had trouble moving his bulk around the court. We won the game 96-85, even playing by Chinese rules and with Chinese referees. Abe was extremely pleased.

But it was a short-lived pleasure. The only game more popular than basketball in China was ping-pong. Abe, the Jewish Community Center champion ping-pong player who had wooed me with his skill the day we first met—and had never lost a match since—took on a twelve-year-old at one of the schools we visited. The boy beat him. Quite a comedown after the other win.

During the day, we visited communes and nursery schools where the children sang "Welcome aunts and uncles!" One evening, we were fortunate enough to be invited to the state dinner Chinese leader Deng Xiaoping held in honor of Vice President Mondale. It seemed that the Chinese leader also loved American basketball.

The 130-proof liquor served at the dinner was a bit overwhelming for our American stomachs, especially since we were supposed to show our appreciation by downing every drop. Since we didn't want to appear unappreciative to our hosts, we furtively poured the liquid fire into the nearest potted plant.

In Shanghai, we defeated the local team, 118-80, before a crowd of 18,000. It was an exciting moment. But, since we were in China for the first time, we also were eager to learn and see as much of Chinese culture as possible. Acupuncture had not yet come to the United States and I was fascinated by what I'd read about its practice in China. When I asked our hosts if we could see a surgical procedure performed with acupuncture in Shanghai, everyone in our group—all the players and my husband too—said "No! We'll pass out!"

"Aw, come on, now," I argued, "Be tough! Be strong! You've got to experience this. It's something you may never get a chance to see again!"

Being persistent, I won out and the tour guide arranged it. One early morning, we were to see a lung operation performed without anesthetic—only acupuncture. The doctor greeted us warmly as we walked toward the hospital building where the procedure was to take place.

The interior of the hospital was quite bare, but we were quickly taken to the operating room. They seated all of us in the balcony. Below us, the patient was lying on the table. The room was completely barren and the windows were wide open. There were no machines in the room, just two women working the patient with needles; one was working with needles on his head and another, his feet. In front of his face was a low, white cloth screen to prevent him from seeing the surgeon performing the surgery, and the acupuncturist doing his head was also feeding him orange slices.

When the surgeon took a saw to cut open the patient's chest so the doctor could perform lung surgery, I felt as if I was going to pass out. Not wanting to embarrass the group, I ran out of the operating theater. Fortunately, there was a sofa in the hallway. I couldn't get there fast enough.

No one followed me. I was the only one who left. After I recovered, I was completely embarrassed. Everyone who had expressed their fears about seeing acupuncture stayed and watched the operation, including my husband. They were fascinated, and I became the butt of their jokes. I had made such a fuss about not being a sissy, but I was the only one unable to watch. I was glad I had insisted; the group never stopped talking about the surgery after we got home.

On our way home from China, we stopped off for another first—the first NBA team to play in the Philippines. It seemed that they loved basketball even more than the Chinese.

So much so that our plane was met by a large woman dressed up to be the "fat lady." This lady didn't sing, but she was assigned to stick by us, particularly Wes Unseld, during our entire visit. That evening, we were invited to the palace for dinner and dancing.

Imelda Marcos, wife of Philippine President Ferdinand Marcos, was an incredible dancer, so naturally, I urged Abe to dance with her, another story he would tell many times. I kept President Marcos company. After the dancing, Imelda—who was still going strong—invited us downstairs in the palace, where she had a disco room. Her night was just beginning, but we had a game the next day.

The next morning, we all received huge bags full of goodies, including capes that she had made for each of the women in our group. Her intention was for us to wear these to the game. When I saw how clumsy and ill fitting they were, I refused to wear mine and suggested the women do the same. Imelda came to the game wearing a gorgeous, red bouclé suit adorned with ruby and sapphire jewelry—our team colors. Did she mean to outshine all of us?

I wondered how she fared in that un-air-conditioned building. But we went home happy. We won again!

Family portrait: Me, at one year, my mom, Goldie and dad, Herman.

Me at age 14 with my dad and my younger sister, Betty

Me with my mother, just home after graduation from U. City High - a month before I met Abe

Abe, just before we met

Me at camp in Pennsylvania the day I met Abe

The night Abe and I got
engaged - 1943

My formal engagement picture –
ring prominently shown

Abe, Linda, and me in
Atlantic City - what a cutie!

My daughter Linda, and her two
brothers, Robert and "Jay Jay"

Abe, Linda, and me

Abe showing off the ceiling height in the
new apartment building, The Irene

Golda Meir, Leah Rabin, Abe, me, and friends

In my office with two favorite patients

The day we bought the Bullets and became sole owners

Our first trip to Russia. Scouting an Ice Show for the Capital Centre and hockey players for the Caps.

Meeting the Pygmies in the Congo

"Irinishka" meets my aunt in Zhlobin for the first time

Abe and me with the Bee Gees at the Capital Centre

With my two great sons, Robert and Jimmy. Lucky me!

I loved dancing with Abe

Our first grandchild Emma

Dancing with "Big" Wes Unseld

*The Big "E" – Elvin Hayes –
my buddy!*

*A fantastic day in Peking - with the
World Champion Bullets*

The World Champion Bullets in Peking

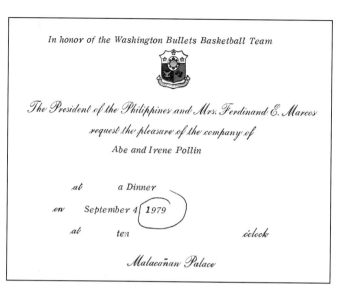

In honor of the Washington Bullets Basketball Team

The President of the Philippines and Mrs. Ferdinand E. Marcos

request the pleasure of the company of

Abe and Irene Pollin

at   a Dinner

on   September 4 1979

at   ten   o'clock

Malacañan Palace

Invitation to the Bullets to visit President and
Mrs. Marcos in the Philippines

With Wilt "The Stilt" Chamberlain. He really was that tall!

My son Jimmy, Abe, President Carter and me at a Hawks vs. Bullets game

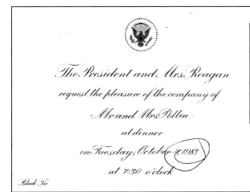

The President and Mrs. Reagan
request the pleasure of the company of
Mr and Mrs Pollin
at dinner
on *Tuesday, October 4, 1983*
at 7:30 o'clock

Black Tie

On the occasion of the visit of
His Excellency
The President of the
Federal Republic of Germany
and Mrs. Carstens

*Invitation to the White House
from President and
Mrs. Reagan*

*President Reagan, Vice President Bush and friends
at a rodeo at the Capital Centre*

*Jimmy Stewart and Ed McMahon at the Reagan Inaugural Gala
that we hosted at Capital Centre*

Welcoming Asaf into our family as my Granddaughter Hannah's husband

*Me and Abe when I received
an honorary PhD from
Howard University*

*A bobble-head of Sister to Sister
Organization "Spokes-robot" –
Holly Heart*

*My big, winning moment
at the NBA Lottery
in 2010.*

THE WHITE HOUSE

April 15, 1994

Irene and Abe Pollin
Two Goldsboro Court
Bethesda, Maryland 20817

Dear Irene and Abe:

    I interrupt this letter to say
"thanks!": thanks for your extraordinary
expression of support in the New York
Times ad of March 29. I was surprised,
heartened and buoyed by this effort and am
deeply grateful.

    Most importantly, thank you for being
our friend and for sharing the goals of
this Presidency. We will prevail.

    With gratitude and kind regards, I
remain

              Sincerely yours,

              Hillary
              Hillary Rodham Clinton

Thanks for everything

Thank you note from
First Lady Hillary Clinton

Thank you note
from President Clinton
following a visit to
MCI Center

THE WHITE HOUSE
WASHINGTON

January 29, 1998

Irene Pollin
One Harry S. Truman Drive
Landover, Maryland 20785

Dear Irene:

Thanks for the great photos. I love them! It
was a terrific time.

Hillary and I send our best to you and Abe, and
we'll hope to see you soon.

    Sincerely,

    Bill Clinton

CHAPTER FOUR

Does life begin at 60?

I was beginning to feel it definitely did—especially for someone who got her Master's Degree at age 50! I felt I'd dropped twenty years off my life by going back to school. As I approached my sixtieth birthday I was on a high; excited and emboldened by the connections I was making in my field and the way my professional life seemed to be taking off.

I'd had to hire two additional social workers at the Neurology Center to help with the influx of patients the doctors were referring. I trained them to do the short-term therapy that I had developed for the chronically ill and their families, and we were having an extraordinary success rate. In fact, we were doing so well that I hoped to expand the practice to include all chronic diseases, not just those with neurological causes. But when I suggested it to Dr. Korengold, he did not want to include patients suffering with other illnesses. I understood, but at that point in my life and work I needed to move forward. I was, and am, forever grateful to him for giving me the opportunity to test my ideas. The next step for me was to open my own clinic, one that specialized in working with all chronically ill patients.

I had managed to heal a bit. The gratification I received from the work I was doing was making a difference. A parent never gets over the loss of a child. The pain never goes away—there are always momentary flashes—but with time the intensity changes. Eventually, I think, you absorb it as part of your psyche. You realize that terrible, terrible things happen to people, but learning to deal with them can lead to growth. As a therapist, I certainly knew that well. And at this stage of life I knew that losing my daughter Linda had made me into a different person. But like other life experiences, it had expanded me, enabled me to understand and help other people in ways I found fulfilling. Yes, I had lost Jay Jay too, but Linda's loss was greater because she was with us for sixteen years. What I had learned in caring for Linda, I now could put to use; it was the basis for helping anyone coping with a life-long illness.

It was also a good time for Abe and me. We were pursuing activities together we both enjoyed—the goings-on at Capital Centre and international travel. We traveled mostly in the summer because in the fall and the winter the teams were playing and we wanted to be home. Aside from trips to exotic places like Tibet, where you had to travel with a group, we rarely traveled with others. "Just the two of us," Abe would say when we took out the atlas. Luckily, we enjoyed traveling and sharing any adventure we could create. And we created some special ones.

For all these reasons, the future was looking very bright for both my worlds—professional and personal. But blue skies can quickly be marred by fast-moving clouds. No one is ever prepared for that sudden change.

Abe had long had a problem with high cholesterol. When he was first diagnosed in the 1960s, he participated in an NIH study testing a medication: cholestyramine powder. Fortunately, the medication worked; his cholesterol went down. In fact, it worked so well that he continued to take it at the doctor's recommendation until the end of his life, even though there were newer drugs. It wasn't much fun to drink six glasses of water several times a day filled with a thick powder, but knowing how it worked helped him swallow it. He learned not to complain. He was feeling great and feeling grateful.

One wonderful warm sunny day in 1980, after a game of tennis, a cardiologist friend noticed that Abe's color had changed. "Abe, you might want to get checked out," he suggested.

Abe stayed overnight at the National Heart, Lung, and Blood Institute, and had an angiogram. "You are going to need a quadruple bypass," Dr. Robert Levy, the director and a friend of ours (a big hockey fan), told Abe. We were shocked. Abe was slim, athletic, and ate healthy foods. "But I have no symptoms!" Abe argued.

"All the more reason to be grateful we found the blockages in time," Dr. Levy said. "I suggest you have the heart bypass at the Cleveland Clinic and have Dr. Floyd Loop do the procedure."

"When?"

"As soon as you can."

"We're in the middle of both the basketball and the hockey seasons," Abe protested. "Can't it wait?"

"I wouldn't take the chance, but it's up to you." Dr. Levy was an internationally known scientist. We were lucky to have his opinion. "If you're going to keep attending these games, though, you better have someone watching you," he told Abe. "You need someone who's knowledgeable about your condition and heart disease in general, sitting right there next to you."

"Like who?" Abe asked.

"Like me," he said with a smile. He could now go to more hockey games.

In the car, we were both silent for a long time trying to absorb what we had just heard. We were familiar with heart surgery and what could happen.

"We're not telling anyone about this," Abe announced, suddenly.

I looked up at him, confused. "What are you talking about?"

"I don't want my mother to worry."

What? I would never understand his relationship with his mother. "Well, then you don't have to tell your mother. But surely we could tell..."

"No one. No one can know until it's over."

"Well, in the office, they'll certainly..."

"No one. I don't want you to tell a soul."

I stared out the window thinking things I couldn't say out loud. *What if something goes wrong? How can I keep this inside, keep the fears unspoken? What a terrible burden this is for me!*

"Do I have your word?" he asked.

"Yes." Abe's way of dealing with things was completely different from mine. But this was his surgery, after all. I had to respect that.

That three-month period felt like three years. Abe not only kept the secret; he seemed to forget it completely. Amazingly, he continued his usual routine of work, watching his teams play, and life at home as though oblivious to what lay ahead. And we continued going to games with Dr. Levy sitting in his seat between Abe and me.

This was an extremely difficult time. Keeping this scary information inside was torture; it was not my modus operandi. Why was he keeping it secret? Was it really so his mother wouldn't worry? Or was his mother an excuse for his way of blocking things that were unpleasant?

It was certainly easier for Abe if no one knew. That was his coping method, but not mine. Once again, I was struck by how differently Abe and I dealt with feelings. His way was to keep things inside, mine to confront, to discuss. Those months were some of the most difficult of my life.

Fortunately, there was a good ending. The surgery, performed at the Cleveland Clinic by Dr. Loop, went perfectly and Abe did extraordinarily well. In fact, he did so well that he was able to attend the 1980 NBA All-Star game at Capital Centre, which was played within weeks of the surgery. He was one determined guy. I always admired that about him.

Searching for a place where Abe could recuperate, I rented a small house on the beach in Barbados. It was perfect. He was able to take long walks daily along the water, waiting for the moment when his doctor told him he could go in again. On returning one morning, he excitedly told me that he was now a member of the "big zipper club." He had just run into another man with the same big zipper scar doing the same walk. This surgical procedure allowed him to live a full and active life.

We did live a full and active life. As a major part of the Washington business community, we were included in almost everything important that was going on.

Ronald Reagan defeated President Jimmy Carter in a landslide in the 1980 election, winning 46 of the 50 states in what was a huge upset to us and to all other Democrats. And yet, in 1981, after the Reagans moved into the White House, Abe and I were invited by telegram to attend a cocktail party at Blair House on the Friday after Election Day. The President and First Lady-elect wanted to get to know members of the Washington community, and as the owners of the local basketball and hockey teams and the Capital Centre, we were an important part of the whole community.

There were about 40 guests, mostly "core" Washington players (those whose lives and livelihoods were not changed by the comings and going of administrations), including the Bishop of the National Cathedral, the directors of the National Gallery and the American Film Institute, the publisher of *The Washington Post*, the president of Howard University, the music director of the National Symphony, and the owner of the Baltimore Orioles.

Interestingly, most of those in attendance were Democrats. Even though Democrats have long predominated in Washington, it was a remarkable gesture on the part of the Reagans to reach out to all the leaders of the community. Everyone in attendance agreed. It turned out this was just the beginning of a sophisticated effort on the part of the Reagans to cultivate Washingtonians. No other administration since has been as successful.

It wasn't long after the Reagans hosted us at that event that we had the opportunity to host them—and at a much bigger one. The 1981 Inaugural Gala was held at Capital Centre. It was a phenomenal event with Johnny Carson, Ethel Merman, Jimmy Stewart, and many other celebrities. The Reagans were Hollywood people, after all, and they knew how to put on a show. Abe and I, of course, attended all the events. It was thrilling to be a part of this happening; we loved every minute of it. I even had a Republican friend from San Francisco staying with us who was involved in the day-to-day planning. Every night, we sat on her bed while she filled in all the details. What fun!

This Inaugural Gala was a first in Washington. There had never been a building large enough to host that size and kind of event. It was all televised. Washington had reached the big time in entertainment. The gossip was that Dean Martin had gotten very drunk before he was to go on, and everyone was worried about what would happen. Frank Sinatra saved the day by convincing Martin he had already sung and had been marvelous. I don't know where Martin spent the rest of the evening.

Waiting for the events to begin, Abe and I had the opportunity to chat with Reagan's press secretary, Jim Brady. It seemed that he was a major hockey fan. All of us were in high spirits, and made elaborate plans for Jim and his family to attend future Capitals games, which sadly, was not to be. Just two months later Brady was shot in the assassination attempt on President Reagan.

True, we didn't lay down the flooring or raise the baskets, and we had hundreds of trained staff doing the real work, like moving sets and cameras. But Abe and I always were the host and hostess of that building, welcoming people as they arrived, making sure everything went off as planned. Our suite was our "living room." This was a large party to host, but host we did with the greatest of enthusiasm.

There were a number of select parties for special guests and we were always included. And, I must admit, I enjoyed getting dressed that night, wearing my hair up, which I never did, and wearing a beautiful, gold lame, two-piece dress. It was glamour at its best.

My daytime life was not as glamorous, but exciting in a different way. I had opened my first office at the Irene, the apartment building in Chevy Chase that we built and Abe insisted on naming after me. No one ever had created a clinic specifically geared toward the needs of people coping with chronic illnesses; my clinic was a first. The story was written up in *Newsweek*, and I was getting calls from around the country from people asking if we could create a clinic in their city or help them begin one.

I began interviewing social workers. But not everyone had the skills, experience and, particularly, the personal approach to work with physically ill, sometimes dying patients. I eventually hired a staff of fifteen which I felt was particularly qualified. We saw a full range of illnesses, some quite challenging. The staff had to be able to handle their problems.

Several stand out to me. One day I received a call from a lawyer requesting that I see a patient in a nursing home in a distant suburb. It meant traveling quite a distance from my office, time away, but I was intrigued. The patient was a man completely immobilized by amyotrophic lateral sclerosis (Lou Gehrig's disease or ALS) who wanted to divorce his wife.

I drove a half hour to the nursing home, and the staff directed me to this man's room at the far end of the building. I'd never been in a nursing home before, and I was stunned by what I saw. Two men were lying on twin beds separated by a screen. On the far side of the room was my patient—a tall, young, good-looking man lying perfectly still with a simple sheet covering him.

My patient could neither move nor speak. How I could I work with him? Therapy requires talking. This would be a challenge, but I wanted to figure out how to communicate with him. His eyes were open, and there was something about the brightness I saw that gave me hope. His intelligence and personality came through. The more I learned about his situation, the more determined I became to do what I could for him and his young family.

The man had been a brilliant lawyer, a Yale graduate, married to an equally brilliant economist and they had two wonderful young children. They had everything going for them, until he came down with ALS.

His wife had taken care of him at home until she ran out of steam. She was working full time and managing the children, and having a harder and harder time coping with the strain the demands of his illness were putting on her. He needed to be hospitalized when his illness had progressed to the point where he was unable to swallow, and rather than bring him home after he was stabilized, she arranged for him to go to the nursing home. Unfortunately, she did not discuss this with him or his family beforehand. He and his parents were angry.

Even though they had always been a very close couple, this discussion was too painful. She couldn't bear to tell him and he couldn't ask. Each one was afraid to hurt the other's feelings and communication broke down. This was not unusual for couples coping with chronic illnesses, but few illnesses progress as fast and are as devastating as ALS.

His reaction was fury. He had expected to go home, not to a nursing home. How could she do this? She was the love of his life! For better or worse! What would the children think? It was unforgivable.

On the other hand, what choices did she have? She loved and adored him, but she could not cope with his care, manage the kids, and meet the demands of the job that was supporting them all.

Her real fear was, "If I get sick and my children lose me, that's it! Then what will we do?" She understood clearly what she could and could not handle. Difficult as it was, she made the decision based on very real possibilities. She didn't expect the anger at her decision. How could I help her as well as her husband?

I began meeting with all of the involved parties, including his parents; his father was a doctor. My goal was to have each one see the other's point of view, understand that no one person was at fault, and that ALS was affecting all of them.

What could I do for my patient? The answer came from the extraordinary man himself. He couldn't move or speak, but his mind not only functioned normally, he was brilliant. I was soon talking to him at all of my visits. He had worked out a system for communicating. On the wall behind his bed were letters with numbers, and he'd select a letter by blinking his eyes a specific number of times.

Speaking to him, I needed to look directly at him even though he could not turn his head. And, I didn't want to learn his system of letters and blinking; it would take valuable time. So I had a nurse stand behind me, calling out the letters. It worked. Soon we were connected—mind-to-mind—talking to each other in complete sentences. It was amazing. We became so adept in his system of communicating I often forgot we were not speaking directly.

At one point, he got a computer and was able to control his messages by blinking. This sometimes included some off-color jokes. He knew he wasn't going to recover, he just wanted out of that nursing home. Then he did the most amazing thing: he arranged to move from the nursing home into an apartment with all the equipment and staff he needed. This was a tremendous accomplishment for him; it proved that he still had some control over his life.

I visited him in his apartment until he died a year later. He was an incredible example of living life to the very end, to the fullest extent possible—even when you are unbelievably limited.

Another case dramatized how seemingly small actions could have big results. A psychiatrist friend of mine referred a couple to me. He had been working with them for a couple of years and couldn't move them from their difficult and life-limiting position. He asked if I would give it a try, and again I was challenged. The wife had suffered a stroke several years before.

My first impression of this couple was their closeness. They were an attractive couple in their early 70s. They had never had children and worked together in a public relations business. She was a particular asset as a hostess as they often entertained clients. He adored her.

Since she had suffered the stroke, however, she had completely shut down. She had recovered almost completely, but her voice had changed; it had deepened and had a gravely tone. Even though she appeared the same, she now refused to meet people and spent most of her days "staring out of the window," according to her distressed husband.

He was devastated. Here was this still-beautiful, outgoing woman who loved clothes and would not even go to a department store. What could I do to help them?

He came with her for every visit. I saw them together and separately. Every time I saw him, he cried at the loss of his beautiful wife—his companion and business partner. Why was she hiding?

After several one-on-one visits, she revealed that she hated the way her voice sounded. In fact, she hated it so much she was embarrassed to see people, old friends as well as new. She couldn't bear people to see or hear her as she was, and she couldn't tell her husband the reason. Additionally, the sound of her voice was a constant reminder that she could never be the same person she was before her stroke.

I tried to think of something to help her get back to her life. Then I remembered one of my own experiences: the man in Florida with the fruit stand. He was the first person I told about Linda's heart condition. Because he was a stranger and I would never see him again, it was a way for me to test public reaction to my story without revealing myself to someone I knew. It was safe.

With this story in mind, I suggested my patient go to a department store—any department store where she didn't know the salespeople. "These people have no idea who you are," I told her. "They have never heard your old voice. And hearing your new voice, you will probably never see them again. You can check their reaction."

I also suggested that her husband go with her, but stand behind a dress rack so that neither she nor the saleswoman would see him. I knew she needed his support and this was a way he could be there in the background.

At the next appointment, they came in grinning from ear to ear. It had worked! She'd made the trip to a department store and had done as I had suggested. In fact, she bought a dress from that saleswoman, her first in three years.

Within a few weeks, not only was she going out again and entertaining at home, she had joined a stroke support group and become a main speaker. She was now using her experience to help others with the same problem.

I was particularly pleased that we were able to accomplish this within three months, particularly after she had spent three years with other therapists. By viewing the situation differently from other therapists, we found a practical solution. Her problem was more situational than psychological.

I was still functioning in two completely opposite worlds: my quiet office therapy world during the day, seeing one person at a time; and our raucous, intense evenings surrounded by thousands of screaming fans.

Sometimes, I wasn't sure which world I belonged to, but it was exciting. It made life interesting; the way that the two worlds and the people in them did not interact.

After a while, however, the publicity generated by my Mrs. Abe Pollin's world—the newspaper pictures of the two of us dancing together at a benefit, attending a function at Capital Centre, receiving an award for philanthropy—interfered with how I was perceived professionally. It had taken years of hard work to develop my career as a psychotherapist, and I didn't want my personal life to have an impact on my work with patients. But sometimes it did. I had spent a year putting together a group of teenagers with cystic fibrosis. Planning a successful therapy group is hard work. It requires interviewing each person, hearing his or her particular issues, deciding how those issues would mesh with the others in the group (Would this one work well with that one? Would she stick it out or drop out?), and then figuring out where and when the group could meet at a time and place convenient for everyone. Since most of these young people were not yet driving, there was another problem: their parents also had to be available to bring them and pick them up.

We were ready to begin our sessions, planning to meet in the evenings at the Cystic Fibrosis Foundation. I was excited about what we would be able to accomplish. On the night before we were to have our first meeting, I received a call at home from the nineteen-year-old who was the leader, the one who had helped me choose the participants. "Hi, Mrs. Pollin, this is Paul. I was wondering if we could hold the therapy sessions in the Sky Suite at Capital Centre."

What? And what was I to do? After a year of working closely with him in the offices of the foundation, this is how he saw me? I was disappointed and angry. After all that time, he viewed me as the wife of the owner of Capital Centre instead of the psychotherapist in charge of the group.

I had no choice. I cancelled the project. As long as these young people were only coming to the group as my guests in a suite at a sports arena, the group would not work. I had lost a year of hard work, but I learned I would probably always have a perception problem.

===============

In 1979, I was invited to a small luncheon at Pamela Harriman's house in Georgetown. The purpose was to get funding for an outpatient house for former mental patients in Washington. I accepted because I was familiar with the place; my sister had spent time there after her long stay at Chestnut Lodge.

The outpatient house had been very good to my sister; I was happy to support the facility. I knew Pamela was married to diplomat Averell Harriman, but nothing else about her.

I attended with a good friend. It was a pleasant event and I believed in the cause. When I was ready to leave, I handed a generous check to Mrs. Harriman. I must have made an impression, because in a few weeks, I received a call from Lew Strudler, a young staffer from the National Mental Health Association. I received him in my office, and he asked if I would be interested in chairing a big fund-raiser with Pamela Harriman. It was to be a large ball with many celebrities, including Walter Cronkite and Art Buchwald, as well as Jennifer Jones, the movie star. I was flattered to be asked. The reason I accepted was that I was a mental health professional and had a mentally ill sister. This was definitely my kind of cause, one I wanted to help. The reason they invited me was as a Washington philanthropist. I could separate the two worlds; but the world did not.

Pamela and I worked together on what turned out to be a very successful and glamorous event. Both Art and Jennifer were interested in the cause because they had both been troubled by depression. I'm not sure how Walter Cronkite got involved, but Pamela's social connections were far reaching. Pleased by how successful the event was in raising money for the association, and by how much we'd enjoyed working together, Pamela and

I began socializing. She had begun giving large parties at home several times a week. She was eager to find a role for herself in Washington.

One common cause was the plight of the Democratic Party, which was in bad shape in the wake of Reagan's landslide. In 1981, it was in bad financial shape—two million dollars in debt. I was a member of the Women's Democratic Club, and soon we began to talk about what we could do to help the party.

One day, she told me about a trip she took to the party headquarters. I clearly remember her description of what she found there: broken-down typewriters, shabby office furniture. We were both embarrassed to be a part of such a pathetic group. We began talking about the situation informally until one evening at one of her parties, in one voice, she and I both said, "We really should do something about it!"

The next thing I knew, she called and announced she was putting a group together called "Democrats for the 80s," and wondered if I'd be interested in joining her. I accepted even though I had not considered what time it might require. I had a full-time practice. But it would be a fun challenge. Like Abe, I loved challenges.

Pamela was a very sophisticated hostess. Her parties, receptions, and fund-raisers were exquisite to the last detail. When she invited people, they came. But, she had never done any public speaking. At her first speech at the Women's Democratic Club, she forgot half her speech. She had been married to several prominent men, but she had always been in the background—the socially astute wife beside the distinguished speech-maker. She turned out to be a pretty quick learner, but her greatest skill was hiring good people.

Her best hire was Janet Howard, a former Hill staffer with an inside understanding of Washington, who became the practical, day-to-day manager of "Democrats for the 80s." I was the only other woman on Pamela's committee. Other members were

Bob Strauss, former Chairman of the Democratic National Committee and U.S. Trade Representative under Jimmy Carter; long-time presidential adviser and attorney Clark Clifford; and Harry McPherson, another lawyer and former presidential adviser.

First, we were planning meetings, and then Pamela began holding fund-raisers or "issues evenings" where well-known policy makers, bankers, labor leaders, and elected officials—each representing a different facet of the Democratic Party—would come and talk about the area that was his or her specialty to a hand-picked audience of donors. Listening to famous people amidst splendid surroundings, namely the Harrimans' collection of Picassos, Matisses, and authentic French antiques, proved quite conducive to giving.

People had to contribute. They couldn't come without contributing. No one attended with giving less than $100,000 per evening. By 1983, Pamela had raised enough to give the party a crucial loan to build a media center where candidates could produce subsidized campaign commercials. We had done it; a small but very knowledgeable group organized everything. We had a lot of fun, but I turned out to be a bit of a disappointment. They assumed I could bring in contributions from all the NBA owners, and I believed I could too, except we miscalculated. It turned out the NBA owners, by and large, were Republicans. The fact that this surprised me shows how unsophisticated I was at the time.

"Democrats for the 80s" became power central, however. By this time, my work and my life dominated my time, but it was the beginning of the modernization of the Democratic Party.

==============

Abe and I had an anniversary coming up and we decided that we would celebrate in the middle of the country: halfway between Riverside, California, where Robert and his family lived, and Washington. We chose Chicago. Robert, Sigrid and their two daughters, Emma and Hannah, came; Jimmy, Abe and I met them at the hotel.

We had a wonderful time doing all the Chicago things—trips on the lake, the museum to see baby chicks hatching—but the highlight of the trip was a Chicago Bulls game. Emma and Hannah, ages ten and twelve, couldn't stop squealing "Michael Jordan! Michael Jordan!" The major treat for them was meeting Michael Jordan backstage. They were ecstatic. He could not have been more charming, and patiently posed for a picture with two little blond, wide-eyed girls. One day in the future, we were to spend a lot of time with Michael—backstage, front stage, everywhere.

=============

"Don't worry about it, Mom. Everything will be fine."

After Abe's father died, Abe's mother called him several times a day, every day.

He was the good son, always her favorite—the daughter she never had, she liked to say. I listened as he patiently tried to assure her about her latest issue. I also thought about the toll of being the "good son."

The only thing I was sure of as I listened to this lengthy, needy phone call was that it was the last thing Abe needed at the moment. This was a difficult business time.

My husband was a very good businessman, but running an arena and owning two teams was proving to be quite a challenge, even for him. The Bullets were playing mediocre basketball and finishing with losing records, and a decade after he'd gotten the franchise, the Capitals had still never made the playoffs. The press was coming down hard on him, and this was very difficult for Abe to take. No one was more focused on his public image. He was very proud of his reputation; he guarded it carefully and constantly.

He was also loyal to a fault. This made him refuse to make some personnel changes on the teams that newspaper columnists and fans were calling for.

It was hard for me too. He could not, would not, talk about his frustrations and feelings. He could talk about the facts—the plays and the players, and finances—but feelings were always off limits.

In addition to their depressing win-loss ratio, the Capitals were bleeding money. Abe had tried countless gimmicks to enhance attendance, but people still weren't coming to games. What's more, television advertising was where the big revenues came from and hockey wasn't on television. Abe had spent time, effort, and money bidding on a potentially lucrative cable TV franchise in hopes of getting those revenues, only to lose out in the end. He had begun selling off some of our assets, buildings we'd built in Washington, to pay off losses.

Finally, in desperation, he issued an ultimatum. To stay in the area, he needed a tax break from Prince George's County, ten sell-out games for the next season, and a much bigger base of season ticket holders. Otherwise, he'd have to sell off or disband the Capitals.

That led to a "Save the Caps" campaign, started spontaneously by a group of ardent fans, led by Steve Mehlman, at the time the director of public relations for the American Association of Retired Persons, and a man who knew how to publicize causes. Soon there was an on-air telethon selling Caps tickets, and local businesses were putting "Save the Caps!" signs atop their newspaper advertising copy. The local chapter of the Special Olympics announced it would use tax-deductible contributions to buy Caps tickets and *The Washington Post* not only ran editorials supporting the cause, but also guaranteed to buy all unsold tickets for one of the Caps' first ten home games. Nine other businesses matched *The Washington Post*'s pledge, thereby setting a team record for consecutive sell-outs, and the Prince George's County Council gave Abe the tax break he wanted. The base of season ticket holders, unfortunately, fell below Abe's goal.

It was enough to keep the Capitals in Washington. But though it slowed the flow of red ink, it did not halt it. Abe sold a small interest in the team to three local investors in hopes of stemming his losses, but that was only a stopgap measure.

For the first time in our married life, I worried about his mental state. Abe was a very competitive man, accustomed to winning and losing, but the present situation was draining his energy and his money. If I asked, "Are you all right?" his answer always was "I'm fine." No more discussion.

In my daytime life, I was having an opposite experience. The Medical Crisis Counseling model had developed into a successful way for treating patients and families coping with long-term illnesses. I was able to treat an increasing number of men and women coping with a range of chronic illnesses within the three-month period I had devised as an appropriate time to help them come to terms with their conditions. I always set a "reachable goal." This was not meant to be a long-term solution; it was meant to help them reach the next stage in acceptance.

I wanted to train others in this model, and contacted the University of Maryland School of Social Work in Baltimore. They were eager to create a training program, but needed funding. Here is where my two worlds came together for the first time in an interesting and valuable way. I came up with the idea of a fund-raiser at Capital Centre called "Sports A-Poppin." It would be a fashion show with a twist, using all of the players of the then three professional sports teams in Washington—football, basketball, and hockey—showing sports clothes. The men would then escort the women—my friends—down the runway with the local sportscasters doing the play-by-play.

As time passed, the event became more and more complicated. We had white swallows flying over the guests and a man and woman riding white horses bareback accompanied by the University of Maryland band playing in the background. It was an enormous success and everyone wanted to repeat it, but I had other important things to do. It did help me to understand, however, the assets and resources I had at my disposal if I wished to use them for a good cause. We raised the money we needed for the program and everyone had fun. I had to get back to work.

Meanwhile, Abe was busy with a new venture. For the first time in a long time, I found him upbeat, excited.

"Video conferencing," he tried to explain. "It's a system that uses audio and video technology to bring people at different sites together so they can see each other and talk to each other as though they were right there together in the same room."

"Like a television telephone?" I asked.

"Sort of. But this isn't necessarily just for people at two locations. It could be many locations at the same time."

"And this company that your buddy is suggesting…"

"Avelex," he said. "That's the name: Avelex."

"Standing for…" "Who knows!" he laughed. "It's just a high-tech sounding name as far as I can tell. But they're putting together this system for video conferencing, and they are very hopeful that it's going to work. And, if they succeed, this could be a really important first."

I smiled at the thought of Abe and yet another "first." Oh, how he loved being the first.

"It is only recently that the transmission networks needed for this kind of technology came into being. It's very new, very cutting edge. They're excited about it. More than just excited. They are pretty certain it will work."

This was the old Abe—positive, excited, hopeful. I was happy for him to have something that gave him a lift during this difficult time in our other businesses.

"Where are they working on it?" I asked.

Like so many of the new technology start-ups: in a garage. "That's where a lot of these new innovations are taking place. This is the

'80s, Irene, the age of technology! On Route 128 around Boston there are many, many entrepreneurs creating new inventions in garages! This just happens to be a garage in Washington. I think it's worthy of investment."

Now, I had enormous respect for my husband's business acumen. He was smart and careful. I trusted his judgment completely. That was his greatest asset, but personally he was totally clumsy about anything mechanical. This may seem odd since he was in the construction business all his life, but he always had someone who was an expert deal with the mechanical and technical sides. The problem was that he was totally dependent on their opinions and judgment.

Too dependent? Maybe. He was also fiercely loyal. The engineer who offered Abe this opportunity to invest in this new technology was an old, high school friend. All I knew was that he was more enthralled than I had seen him in a long time. Abe wanted my support and I gave it. "If you think it's worthy, then go for it!"

He kissed me. This was the first time that Abe was going into something that he didn't know anything about, and was also completely dependent on others. Going into sports was a new business, but it was a business; this was technology. Others were in control. Only time would tell if this was a good decision. I felt trepidation, but kept it to myself.

Rehoboth was always the place we went for brief getaways. But through the years it changed from the easy, quiet place that we loved, to traffic and shopping malls. It was now taking us longer to get to the house and we were going less and less. I suggested to Abe that we try to find a place closer to Washington—one hour away rather than three hours. He said, "Okay, go look. But I want to build something."

This surprised me, but I think it was the old builder in him; he missed building. He said he wanted to build a log cabin on a lake. If I could find such a place, he was all for it. My job was to find that place within an hour from Washington.

I also loved the idea again of finding a location and creating something that was special for us. So I began a several-year search that filled whatever time I had between patients. I did enjoy it. I began by drawing a circle around Washington within a one-hour radius. "A place we could just throw stuff in the car and go to." That was the idea.

I drove around the Washington area, Virginia, and Maryland with real-estate salespeople, but nothing fit the description that Abe outlined. Finally, one Realtor said, "What about Middleburg?"

I hadn't even considered it as a possibility. "That's for horse people. We're not horse people," I said.

"You don't have to be horse people," was her response. I began looking in Middleburg, Virginia and fell in love with the area. It was beautiful, and an hour from Washington. On the first trip, I saw exactly what Abe had wanted—a piece of land, no house, a "lake" (well, it was really a pond) and exactly one hour from Washington.

I couldn't wait to show it to him. He also loved it, especially when he timed the drive to be exactly one hour from our house in Bethesda. Even the price was right. I suggested we buy it immediately. The problem was that we were about to leave for a trip to Scandinavia. There wasn't much time to negotiate the deal, so Abe suggested that we wait until we returned from the trip.

Since I had been the one scouting out possible locations and I knew there was nothing like this anywhere else, I pressed him, "Shouldn't we do it now—just to be sure?"

"Nah," he said. "It will be here when we get back."

We returned from a wonderful trip to Scandinavia and it was gone. He felt awful and I was angry. I had spent so much time looking. I was not willing to devote more time to this project. I was done. I was adult enough to give it up as a lost cause.

But Abe felt enormous guilt. He did not want to give it up and called an agent to pursue the quest. Within a few weeks, he arranged for her to drive us around the area and, of course, there wasn't anything else with a "lake" and no house. And the poor guy felt even guiltier. One late afternoon, after covering a lot of the places I had already seen, we pulled up in front of Cloverland, a house in Middleburg that I thought was the most beautiful thing I'd ever seen. The view from the back was magnificent, overlooking the Blue Ridge Mountains. Every room was just as I had planned in my dreams. There was no pond, no lake, and it wasn't empty land, but it did have a beautiful view. It also had this wonderful house.

"Let's tear this house down," was Abe's first response.

"WHAT?" I shrieked, "You don't tear this house down!"

"Okay, okay" was his quick response. I think it was the guilt, but buy it we did.

It was the exact opposite of what Abe wanted—a small log cabin and a lake—but it was an hour away from our house. The house was not in good shape, but with our construction people, in a short time we were able to bring it to top condition. We redid the landscaping and added a garden that included apple and peach trees, some grape vines, and blueberry bushes. Abe was able to have his beloved tomato plants. And I not only had an enchanted flower garden, but a small greenhouse (restored children's playhouse) to experiment with various plants. It was the perfect getaway.

We began going there as many weekends that we could. Even if we could only get away for the day, we could have lunch there and still be able to drive to the city for an evening game. Because it was so accessible, we could have large family gatherings in the large dining room for Passover and Thanksgiving. Looking out at the Blue Ridge Mountains from every window in the house gave us the kind of peaceful respite that we needed. The contrast was striking between the quiet beauty of Cloverland and the ear-splitting noise of the arena an hour away where our teams played. We both appreciated that "log cabin on the lake."

Months had passed and Avelex, the new video conferencing technology Abe had invested in, was not coming in as promised. Abe was becoming more than a little anxious about it. Each time the technical people gave Abe a firm completion date, it didn't happen. This was extremely difficult for Abe to accept. His business style was the opposite. He kept his word and his promises. When he set dates for completing his building projects, he met them no matter how difficult it was to accomplish.

Each time he went to the garage and looked at the equipment, which he did not understand, they said, "Not ready yet. Almost."

He had to accept their word since he had absolutely no connection to the work they were doing. He trusted them and felt they were doing their best. But he was the one who invested all the funds and he was the one who needed to sell it. Abe was a man that needed control. Now he was in a situation where he was totally without control— dependent upon someone else's performance in an area about which he knew nothing.

He was also a man who was extremely proud of his reputation and guarded it carefully. Now he had been using that sterling reputation to recruit corporate investors, inviting them to come and see this new technology. It soon became a painful and embarrassing experience. Every time he set a date for the demonstration, it had to be canceled, often at the last minute. This was not the way he'd ever done business. His reputation and sense of self were at stake. I hoped and prayed it would come through for him. His investment was not just money, it was his "word."

Meanwhile, my work was expanding.

I was invited by the head of the Washington Hospital Center to help put together a task force to "humanize health care"—to work with hospital professionals on improving patient services. I chaired several conferences that looked into issues like bioethics, increasing support for patients with cancer and patients with kidney transplants or going through dialysis. I was asked to create a whole new department at the hospital to both deal with these social issues and continue the therapeutic work I was doing with chronic disease patients.

It was an amazing opportunity, but, as often happens, it didn't come easily. What hospital administrators thought was a good idea did not sit well with the medical and psychiatric staffs. When the word got out, the psychiatrists and medical doctors protested quite loudly. The psychiatrists were terrified my department was going to take their patients away. After several weeks of very unpleasant gossip, we met to sort things out. I could not understand their resistance. Why would they be against it?

At the meeting, sitting face to face, I told them, "You're going to get *new* patients. I'll be bringing in patients with chronic diseases, and since my model is short-term therapy, three months, any who need more than three months are potential patients for you."

Once they understood the value of my department for them, we were heartily accepted. My Medical Crisis Counseling model was working again. Soon I was training more social workers and the Washington Hospital Center gave me more opportunities to be creative. I was given the chance to develop a counseling center in the new hospital wing. I worked on the concept, but did not stay to open it. Again, another major moment in my professional life occurred. I was invited to write a book about my model for a major publishing company, W.W. Norton. I knew I couldn't do both. I regretted leaving what I had built, but the book offered a larger audience, one that I am pleased is still using it.

Then, miracle of miracles! The Avelex technology seemed to be working. Abe was now ready to invite important major investors to see the first demonstration of video conferencing. We were thrilled. It was all we could talk about on our way to Cloverland the day before. After a quiet dinner and getting ready for bed, the phone rang. I could hear Abe's voice. He was agitated. "I'll be right there."

"Right where?" I asked.

"I have to go Washington. There's a problem," as he started dressing.

"It's eleven o'clock! Can't it wait until tomorrow morning? It's dark to be driving now," I urged. "Please don't go."

Pulling his clothes on as fast as he could, he said, "The Japanese are arriving tomorrow afternoon.

"I have to go. I have to be there. I have a lot on the line. I have to know it's going to work." He ran downstairs and jumped into his car.

I flopped into the nearest chair as I heard the car pulling away in the dark night.

The next day when he returned home, I heard the dreadful news. The Japanese had come and the demonstration failed. He was devastated. He now had to make a decision. Could he continue to support this project? He had so much of himself invested. The strain was beginning to take its toll.

Watching him struggle was very painful for me. I understood what he was feeling, but couldn't do anything to relieve it. I just continued to go to work confident that he would make the right decision at the right time.

My reputation and experience were now opening more doors. I received an appointment to the National Cancer Advisory Board at the National Institutes of Health. This was quite a prestigious board and I felt honored to serve. But what made it unusual for me was that a Republican president, Ronald Reagan, had appointed me. My Democratic credentials were well known.

Being invited to publish *Medical Crisis Counseling* was a triumph after years of hard work on another book, *Taking Charge*. I had no intention of writing a book about anything until some of my book club friends suggested it.

"You should write a book about your work," they said. Many of them were professional writers and editors and offered to help. They had heard about the work I was doing during the many evenings we spent together. One was Ruth Boorstin, wife and editor to her husband, Daniel Boorstin, then the Librarian of Congress. She even arranged a meeting with Si Bessie, senior vice president of Harper & Row, one of the most highly regarded editors in the business. Since I was not of that world, I had no idea when I walked into his office in New York who I was meeting.

He greeted me warmly and I described the work I was doing. Imagine my surprise when he said, "How soon can you write it?"

How long could it take? This was my specialty, after all. Who knew more about it than I did? Thinking about all of the files in my office with patient stories, I said, "Three months."

(It would take me ten years, but, at the time, that seemed a reasonable estimate—especially for someone who had no idea what went into writing a book.)

Things were going well at work, but not on the home front. The teams weren't doing well, Avelex wasn't doing well, and Abe's mother had a stroke and died. The suddenness of her death was a shock. She was eight-six and had been in quite good health. I could not tell how this affected Abe. She had always been a major presence in his life. But Abe, as usual, didn't discuss his feelings. He became even more silent. We always discussed business, but this time he didn't even want to talk about that. He was also in the throes of deciding about Avelex. He was incredibly tense. I tried to get him to talk, but why did I think I could get him to change?

Watching him grow more silent, I thought maybe a few days away with some guys might give him a chance to relax in a different way, although he had never done this. I suggested that this might be a good break for him.

When he agreed, I was pleased and helped him pack. I didn't even ask where he was going. I knew he would call me as soon as he arrived at his destination. But he didn't call. This thoroughly surprised me; it was atypical. I thought, maybe he is having such a good time he will just call tomorrow morning. But he didn't call the following morning or evening.

By then I was getting quite worried. Did something happen to him? I always knew where he was; he always let me know. He called me every night on his way home from work. "Hi Honey, I'll be home in twenty minutes."

I didn't know who to call. I thought I might take a chance and call his office. I asked his secretary if she had a number where he was staying. Her response almost knocked me off my chair.

"No," she said. "He doesn't want to talk to you."

The next day, I learned, Abe called his 200 employees together and told them we were separating. I was the last to hear.

CHAPTER FIVE

What do you do when the world as you knew it suddenly turns upside down?

We were separating? Who decided this? Since when? For what?

Is this the man I'd kissed three days earlier, urging him to relax and have a good time on the trip I'd suggested he take with his buddies? I'd hoped these few days would give him some perspective on his multiple business problems.

This was too crazy. It was not real.

I was in shock—total, unbelievable shock. I couldn't breathe.

We were separating from what? The words had no meaning for me.

I couldn't fathom what that meant. He had never said a word that ever suggested anything about anything. And he didn't want to speak to me? Why not?

Without a doubt, this was the weirdest experience I'd had in my entire life. I had no clue as to any aspect of this situation.

What was I supposed to do? I was at home surrounded by all of the things we had built together. Pictures of our family, places we had gone together over the years—Africa, Tibet, Rehoboth, and Cloverland. When had we fought?

Why were we separating? Can one person say "we" are separating?

After several days, and speaking to many friends, I moved from stunned to anger. How could he do this to me? His best friend, his partner?

Well, screw him! Now I was so angry at him, I would leave him. I would move out of our house, out of our life.

I'd move to Georgetown. I'd get a new house, a new life. This was not my choice, but if that was what he wanted, then so be it. I would adjust. I would show him two could play this game!

This whole time, however, I couldn't stop mulling over the "why" part. Since he never mentioned it to me and wasn't speaking to me, I was stuck with "why?" Being a psychotherapist, I thought and considered and calculated. There had to be a reason. As I thought more clearly, I reviewed Abe's recent behavior. What had been going on in his life that he wasn't sharing with me?

I knew he had been extremely upset of late; that was the reason I suggested that he get away. Some of the issues were his mother's sudden death, the failure of Avelex, the losses the teams were generating, the harsh criticisms of the media, the anger expressed by the fans. I'd seen him struggling for several years and, as much as I tried to get him to talk about it, he couldn't. I knew that about him; knew that from the day we met. During all our years of marriage, he never could talk about his deepest feelings, including talking about the losses of our children. The days away with some old buddies I thought might get him to relieve some of those deeply hidden emotions. But it still didn't help me to understand why he said we were "separating" and why he couldn't speak to me? Why didn't he want to face me?

Did he feel ashamed to tell me the extent of the losses? Or was I not available because I was too busy with work? He had been selling off a number of our properties to cover the losses, which I knew. But did he feel that I didn't agree with that?

Had he kept so much turmoil bottled up inside that it had all just exploded and he'd found himself unable to cope? Was this some sort of "walking breakdown?"

Hoping that his brother Harold, who I had been close to for many years, might give me some idea of the "why," I called him.

I never forgot his answer. "He doesn't love you and he doesn't like you." I remember being proud of my response. "Harold, you don't know what love is." He had been married and divorced twice. I knew that he was envious of Abe's and my long relationship.

The true answer continued to remain elusive because Abe refused to talk and meet—except in a psychiatrist's office.

He was seeing a psychiatrist. I was seeing a psychiatrist. After several months, he told me his psychiatrist suggested we wait a year before getting back together. But, by now, I had had enough time to realize how crazy this all was for me.

"I don't think so," I said. "You go on with your life, and I'll go on with mine."

And good riddance. I'm fine by myself. I don't need this!

But the truth, of course, was that I wasn't fine by myself. I loved him. The more I thought, the more certain I was that I didn't want to lose any more people in my life. I had lost my infant son, my daughter, my parents, and my sister. I was willing to do anything not to lose another person I loved. Abe was my family. I could not lose him.

We began to meet more often in the offices of both of our psychiatrists, and sitting as far away as possible on the couch, began to open up more of a dialogue. In my psychiatrist's office one afternoon, Abe suddenly blurted out that he had not wanted our daughter Linda to have the surgery that had cost her her life, and that I had been the one who had pushed for it.

I was shocked. This was 25 years after the fact. All three of us had discussed that decision for months, all of us sitting on the bed in our bedroom. "But we all made the decision together," I said, my heart pounding as I almost passed out.

"Yes, that's true," Abe said. "But I didn't want her to have it. I've often thought she might still be alive if she hadn't had it."

Had he been feeling that way all these years, keeping these thoughts closed off?

I had gone through hell for ten years after Linda died with Abe there to support me, and he had felt this way? Had he kept the pain and anger inside him all that time? Why now?

I never found out.

At Abe's request, after a few months, we started "dating." He would come to the house and take me out, and then bring me back home. How strange for him to put his key in the door and let me in and for him to get back in the car and drive away.

Then, during one session, my doctor suggested that long walks might be a good idea. It was something Abe and I liked to do.

And so we walked and walked and walked on the C&O Canal path near our house, day after day, hour after hour, for weeks. I now began to feel like Abe's therapist, but all that came out was that he was "just unhappy."

One day I got so frustrated I told him that I wished there were a kind of mental enema I could give him to get his feelings out. He liked my enema line, but we still talked about all the things we had always talked about. The cause of the separation never surfaced.

And then, at Abe's request, he moved back into the house. This, however, proved to be premature. He really wasn't ready. He was still very angry. Suddenly, everything became a negotiation, a debate. He had never been like that before. I just couldn't handle any more.

"I can't deal with this. Please go," I said. This time I was so angry, I took all of his clothes, put them in the garage, and said, "You send someone over here for this!"

Not long after that he returned and, gradually, we went back to our life together as it had been. Within a few weeks, we went to California to visit Robert and Sigrid, and their children, Emma and Hannah. It was as if nothing had ever happened. We had a wonderful visit. Again, we began to enjoy each other's company. We had always had fun together. We even found humor in the few awkward moments. How could this ever have happened?

There was never an answer to the mystery of "why?" The closest we came was one night, in the hotel, as we were about to fall asleep, Abe suddenly admitted, "I have a hard shell around me to keep anyone from getting too close."

I was shocked to hear him admit this, but it did help me to understand why, throughout our lives, he could never discuss anything painful. He had learned to keep all of his feelings inside; something I could never do or understand. I always knew that about him, but hearing him say it erased any questions that I might still have about why.

Before I was only guessing. Now I clearly understood. And understanding helped me not to press him. I loved him the way he was. In my book *Taking Charge*, I used the terms "confronters" and "avoiders" based on two opposite personalities. I liked facing the facts head on, whereas he avoided facing the facts head on. The way that our marriage relationship worked is that I avoided pushing him to face facts head on, confronting him, and he appreciated that.

===============

When my father died in 1963, three months after Linda, my mother continued to write to his sister, Bobtse, in Russia. Although he never saw her again, he had never lost touch. Then when my mother died suddenly of a heart attack the following June, I continued the correspondence. This was not easy for me since I knew no Russian and had totally forgotten any Yiddish I had learned as a youngster. My only alternative was to get a translator, which I did, and was able for a time to continue the relationship. Her letters were warm and she reported mostly personal things: her health and that of her children, and wanted to know the same from me.

I had difficulty sticking to this regimen. I was incredibly curious now that I had this opportunity to learn about life in the Soviet Union. What it was like living in a Communist country in 1964? I never considered what it required of her. I was totally ignorant of what daily life was like for her, her family and anyone living in that country at that time. Even though I had read that people there were restricted in their speech and activities, even jailed and sent to Siberia, I just couldn't believe it. My curiosity got the better of me, and then I began, with each letter, asking for more and more details. Having grown up in such a different country, I simply could not accept the fact that the kind of freedom I took for granted was not available to people who lived in other societies. Our mutual correspondence lasted for several months and then suddenly it stopped. At first, I was worried that something happened to her health. The real reason never occurred to me. I continued to write but no return letters.

I finally stopped. The reason she had stopped writing finally dawned on "stupid, ignorant" me. I had pressed her for information she could not give. Why should she put her life and that of her family at risk to answer my naïve, but to her "dangerous," questions?

I never stopped thinking about her and her family. In 1974, when Abe and I went to Russia to negotiate for some hockey players, I sent a telegram to her address, asking her to contact me at my hotel. Again, there was no response.

I was terribly disappointed, but I finally had to conclude that she was dead. I would no longer try to contact her.

Abe had been disappointed on that trip too. He had hoped to visit the small village his parents had come from—Korostyshev. Our travel guide, a young, attractive, blond woman who we were certain was a KGB agent, had promised she would arrange the visit. Several days passed, and no trip. We continued to make the request, and she finally said that she would take us there the next day. The next day, however, she reported that it was impossible for her to take us there, but if we wished, she would show us what a village like that was like. It was close to Moscow and we could go that afternoon. Abe was determined not to be put off, and told her we would sit in the hotel lobby until she came by with the car and driver.

Sitting in the lobby for hours, she returned several times telling us that she wasn't sure she could do as promised. By this time, Abe was livid.

He said, "No. That does it. I'm sitting here. I'm not leaving this hotel lobby until you take us there."

We continued to sit in the lobby until it was beginning to get dark, but he would not move. Embarrassed in front of the other people in the lobby, she finally said, "All right. I'm going to take you to see a village."

The three of us drove in a black sedan about a half hour out of the city to what appeared to be the suburbs. She pointed to one side of the road and said, "See, there's the village like your parents."

We didn't know whether to laugh or cry. We were tired and hungry, not in a mood to be duped. That's when we both became determined to one day return to Russia and see our parents' villages and towns.

"Only next time," I told Abe, "we will have our own American translator. We won't depend on them."

That is why in 1989, when Abe negotiated a deal to bring the Capitals hockey team to the Soviet Union, he specified we would come only if Soviet authorities allowed us to go visit the places our parents had come from. And, this time, we would bring our own translator—Katherine Young, a young American woman who was translating for the team.

And off we went! First stop for the hockey team was Sweden, where they played several games, then on to Riga and Moscow. Buoyed by the Capitals' 8-7 win in overtime against Moscow's Spartak hockey team, we left the team's tour and set out to visit the villages and towns our parents came from. First traveling to Kiev, which would be our home base, we began an hour's drive west to Korostyshev, Abe's parents' village, but this time with an entire retinue. Our group included Katherine, her colleague, Sergei, a driver, and a helper, in addition to Abe, my brother-in-law, Harold, and me. We were determined to discover as much as we could about our families.

Driving into Korostyshev one early morning, the first thing we saw was a flower market with just a few people mingling around. We stopped and asked an elderly woman if she knew the name Polonofsky. Her response was unexpected. "Yes," she said. "Where do they live?" She pointed to a house on a nearby street, and we all headed in that direction. This was a place that had not changed very much in the 75 years since Abe's mother and father had left for America. This was "Fiddler on the Roof" territory—a small Russian village with cows slowly making their way down the mud streets.

We knocked on the door of the house, asked for Polonofsky, and were told to go next door. Our excitement was palpable. When we knocked on that door, a young dark-haired woman answered, "Yes" when we asked, "Polonofsky?"

Taken aback but reassured by the sight of our Russian friends, this woman, Julia, invited us into her home. She excused herself, telling us she wished to find her father, and told us to make ourselves at home. Within five minutes, she returned with a man in his fifties, who looked amazingly like Abe's father. He ordered his daughter to bring us food and drink. While she began preparing potato latkes and serving glasses of vodka, he proceeded to give us the background of the village and the family.

Mr. Polonofsky had spent his entire life in this tiny Ukrainian village on the bank of the Teterev River. During World War II, the town lost 60 percent of its Jewish population. He began showing us pictures of his grandfather and other relatives several generations back. We could see the facial similarities, even the cleft chin of our uncle, Dan Pollin. Mr. Polonofsky had lost track of many of his relatives who had moved to Chicago in the 1920s.

He then insisted that we accompany him to the cemetery where his parents were buried. He was a bit embarrassed. It was a Catholic cemetery. He and his family had given up their Jewish identity.

Back to the house, feeling very relaxed after the vodka and latkes, I said to Julia, "Let's check if your father is really a Pollin."

"What do you mean?" she asked curiously.

"Well," I said. "There are definite family traits. Is he kind of stubborn and hard-headed?" I knew of what I spoke, because I knew all Pollin men, including my husband, brother-in-law, father-in-law, uncle, and the five brothers.

Not surprised, her answer was, "Absolutely!"

"Okay, then," I laughed. "He must be a Pollin."

"Now that we've met and reunited," Abe said as we were preparing to leave, "You have to root for the Washington Capitals during tomorrow's game in Moscow!"

But true to the Pollin legacy, his response was, "Absolutely not. I'm rooting for my team, Dynamo Moscow!"

Abe got a kick out of that. With very warm feelings, we left with promises to stay in touch. We needed to return to Kiev. The next day we were going to drive to my father's town, Zaslav, which was about an hour farther west.

Early the following morning, our group took off on our next adventure. The difference was that Sergei and Katherine had done some reconnaissance and we were expected. On a beautiful, fresh fall morning, we drove into what had probably been a beautiful, small administrative town. The streets were wide with rows of trees down the middle. Houses were set back off the street. Even though the town looked neglected, remnants of the old elegance still remained.

We drove up one of the main streets and parked our van in front of one of the houses. Katherine and Sergei led Abe, Harold, and me up to this house and rang the doorbell. No response. A few minutes passed. They rang again. This time, they also knocked on the door to the screen porch, but more silence. Katherine and Sergei were dumbfounded. He had been to this house and met with the family. They were expecting us. What could have happened? Katherine made a suggestion.

Why don't the men go back to the van and only Irene and I try to get a response? She understood that the family could be terrified of this group, particularly the big, tall Russian driver and his helper. Even though Sergei had been greeted warmly when he last visited, he had not calculated their fear of being seen speaking to visiting Americans.

The men left Katherine and I alone, standing at the bottom of four steps leading up to the door of the screened porch. We again rang the bell and could see in the shadows someone peering at us through the screens. The door opened and a middle-aged woman appeared. She reached down, touched my face, and said, "You look just like a Kirchik!" I was breathless.

I couldn't move until her husband appeared behind her and invited us into the house. We called out to the group sitting in the car, and soon we were all greeted warmly into their sparsely furnished but comfortable home. The living room was lined with books. Her husband, we later learned, was a journalist. There was a television set, a small sofa, one lamp, another table with the telephone on it, and two wooden chairs. They even showed us their root cellar where they stored bushels of potatoes for the winter.

They served us tea and told us the recent history of Zaslav. It seemed that, during the war, their house had been used as a Nazi headquarters. Miraculously, they had been able to return.

They wanted to connect us to the Kirchik family, and walked us next door to their neighbors, who they said knew the Kirchiks. Her husband walked us through a small garden and into another small, spotless cottage with sparkling white lace curtains. Again, we were greeted warmly. Not only did they know the family well, they were in touch with my cousin, Frida, who currently was living in Kiev. By this time, we needed to return to Kiev to meet our train. They wrote down Frida's address in Kiev and we ran to the van. Why hadn't they mentioned this earlier? We had no time to learn anything but a phone number and address.

I stayed in touch with this family for several months, exchanging letters, and even received the husband's beautiful poetry. The information they gave us opened a whole world for another Kirchik family.

Meeting all of these people was a feeling that is difficult to describe. They were very much alive, living in the same present as we were but surviving something we could not identify with. I wondered what it had been like for my mother and father to grow up in that area. My father's family was quite comfortable in the hotel business. My mother's family, children of a rabbi, lived nearby in a small village named Triesk. The stories I heard from both of them were of a good life, pretty village and town with a river they often swam in, until what had become a common occurrence—groups of soldiers racing through the streets looking for Jews, and their hiding under the stoves.

Gradually, over several generations, the family left in small groups to established family in St. Louis, Missouri, where they could live without fear. They didn't leave to better their economic lives; they had been comfortable. They wanted freedom to be themselves. I feel sure that is one of the reasons so many of these teenagers, including my parents, leaned toward socialist ideals soon after they arrived in the United States. They could, for the first time, be free to express what they actually felt.

Having these experiences in one's life is so extraordinary. I am eternally grateful. It made me feel so connected to my past, but my curiosity was still not completely fulfilled. I still had never heard anything definitive about my Aunt Bobtse, even though I pressed Sergei and Katherine. One afternoon at home, still feeling the warmth of our experience, my doorbell rang. Katherine was standing there. "I have something for you," she said, handing me a video. "We found your aunt. This is a film of her and her family in Zhlobin that Sergei took last week."

Shaking, I put the video in the slot, placed myself on the sofa in front of the television set. There was my Aunt Bobtse and her family sitting on a sofa with all of my family's pictures on a table in front of her. Katherine, sitting by my side, translated. It was hard for me to get my bearings. I had been looking for her since 1964, when she stopped writing. This was 1990. I had accepted that she was dead, and there she was in front of me, talking to me, showing me pictures of my family that my parents had sent to her over the years. Even in her advanced age, she looked remarkably like my sister and her mother—my grandmother—who had immigrated to America and lived with us for a few years. She had the same high cheekbones and athletic build. Her son, Semyon, showed pictures of my high school graduation, my children, and my niece and nephew; all pictures that my parents had sent over the years.

All the begging and threatening I had been doing the past few years with Sergei and Katherine had paid off. He found a woman in Yalta who knew my aunt and gave him her address in Zhlobin. Katherine asked if I would like to speak with her and, of course, my answer was yes. But how? Katherine walked to the phone, dialed a number, and I heard excited Russian voices. When I heard my Aunt's voice for the first time, I could barely speak. She spoke in Yiddish, and I was able to recall the little I knew. This was only the beginning. I knew I would have to see her and her family as soon as I could.

My first instinct was to invite them to visit us, but my aunt was 83 and had a hip problem. I would have to go see her in Zhlobin. At this point, the opportunity seemed remote except for "fate" or whatever one can call an unexpected windfall. A few weeks later, I received an invitation to accept an International Oncology Award in Hamburg, Germany, at the World Cancer Congress, for my work with cancer patients. I was extremely pleased and honored. More important, this provided me with the opportunity to travel to Zhlobin. Abe was just as thrilled as I was, but said that he had to be back in Washington within ten days. If we could make that work, it was a go.

Making arrangements to follow through on this plan proved to be next to impossible. This was 1990. Gorbachev had introduced Glasnost and an easing of some restrictions, but the Iron Curtain was still in place. It took months of hard work by our two translators, one in Washington and one in Kiev, our patient travel agent, and even a friend at the Soviet Embassy in Washington the day before we left. The problem was, Abe was in the middle of a major business transaction and could only get away for a few days. The Soviets thought it was a little strange for Americans to make such a long trip for just a few days.

Part of the "doing" required chartering a small, British, private plane to take us directly from Hamburg to Minsk. If we did not do this, we would have had to travel first to Moscow and then take a train. When we got to Minsk, we'd have to drive four hours to Zhlobin, which was a town of 150,000, but didn't have an airport. We also needed to have a place to stay overnight in Zhlobin.

I also had to fulfill a peculiar request from my cousin Semyon. In a letter proclaiming his joy over our upcoming visit, he'd asked if we would be so kind as to bring a Geiger counter with us.

A Geiger counter? At first I dismissed the whole idea. Where on earth do you buy a Geiger counter? The day before I left I contacted a friend who was formerly in the State Department. He was not at all surprised by my request, and proceeded to look in the Yellow Pages and find a place where I could buy a Geiger counter.

"Is it okay to bring a Geiger counter into Russia?" I asked

"No problem," he said.

If my cousin had asked for one, there had to be a good reason. I bought one that was about the size of a camera, still curious what he wanted it for.

After our three-day stay in Hamburg, as arranged, we boarded a small, seven-passenger jet from a British company known as Chauffair. Greeting us were two handsome British pilots wearing their dark blue uniforms with gold epaulettes on their shoulders. As they told us to fasten our seat belts, they added that they certainly hoped they would be able to find Minsk; they had never been inside Russia before.

We were all game. Several hours later, we landed in a city we hoped was Minsk. The airport personnel who greeted our Citation V plane peered inside, and their jaws dropped. They had never seen a small private jet. "It looks like a toy!" one murmured.

We boarded a bus that took us to several waiting cars, filled with suitcases of Abe's and mine, and those of my son, Jimmy, and my niece, Ilene, who had joined us in Hamburg so they too could meet the family in Zhlobin. We had a lot of baggage, since we were traveling with gifts for the family as well as three cases of Evian water. Having traveled to Russia twice before as well as China three times, I knew that having water with us was an important safety cushion.

In the car on our way to Zhlobin, Sergei told us that we would be staying at the one hotel in the town, which appropriately was called "The Hotel." He hadn't wanted to tell us earlier, but now he admitted there were no showers in the hotel. Never mind, he said, he had made arrangements to shuttle us to a shower.

Well, that wouldn't be too bad. We were only going to be there two nights.

He warned there would be no hot water for washing. Abe began wondering out loud how he was going to shave without hot water. We were in for another surprise when we got to the front desk and the lady there told us that not only was there no hot water, there was *no* water. (Abe innocently asked what time it would be turned on.) I had visions of flushing toilets with Evian water.

But Sergei came though, arranging for someone to bring us buckets of water from the river for toilet flushing. We "washed up" with Evian water as quickly as we could and took off to my aunt's apartment building, a few blocks away.

As we approached the entrance, I recognized Semyon waiting for us. We ran toward each other and hugged, and walked up the two flights of stairs to their apartment. I remember the stairs being strangely uneven—one eight inches high, the next one two inches high. The halls were in terrible condition. The walls were dirty and filled with patched holes. But, once inside the apartment, we found it spotlessly clean. My Aunt Bobtse, using a cane, walked toward us. My first instinct was to run to her and grab her, but I didn't know how steady she was on her feet, so I restrained myself. Instead, I walked slowly toward her as she walked toward me until we met and hugged. At that contact, lights were flashing from the three cameras my family had brought. When Katherine, our American translator, asked earlier if I would cry, I said probably not. I never cry, I told her. I might be choking with emotion and feel pain in my chest, but I wouldn't cry.

Well, I cried. Not hard, but I couldn't restrain the tears of joy that came rolling down my face. Her hug was big and warm, and we held onto each other for several minutes. "Irinishka!" she whispered in Yiddish, "Mine terya kind."

I almost melted right there because that was the expression my father had always used. It meant "My dear child" and not having had that kind of love since my parents died, the diminutive "Irinishka" almost blew me away.

After hanging onto each other for a few minutes, Jimmy came forward and introduced himself, followed by Ilene. Then it was Abe's turn to put his arms around her and introduce himself.

"Abby… Abby!" she cried as she hugged him.

Her warmth and energy were remarkable. I then understood why Sergei had told us that, of all the people he had contacted for us, she was the one he had liked the most. I had never seen a 35-year-old Russian in blue jeans flirt with an 84-year-old lady in a house dress, but the looks that passed between these two were electric. "I've never had anyone like that in my life," he told me. "I was an only child and my parents were divorced. I never knew that kind of charm and caring."

We sat down to a table filled with platters of food and drink—baked chicken and cooked salads as well as traditional Russian Jewish dishes, such as baked stuffed fish. Next came a specially baked chocolate cake, which her granddaughter had decorated with the date—August 21, 1990—on top. Then came a variety of fresh fruits, which they proudly presented, telling us where each one had come from. The peaches were from Georgia, they explained, the watermelons from Yalta.

I thought they were trying to tell us they had gone to a lot of trouble to gather these fresh fruits for this special occasion, but I discovered there was another reason. Their town had been affected by the radioactive clouds blowing from Chernobyl, and they wanted us to know the fruits were not contaminated.

So that's why Semyon wanted a Geiger counter!

As we ate the fruit, I handed my cousin his gift. He was elated. "I will become famous in Zhlobin," he said. "I am the only person in town with this."

We exchanged additional gifts. They had a present for every one of us and for relatives they knew about who were not there. They proudly gave us boxes and dolls that were from Zhlobin, and also personal medals they had earned. One was a coin with the years 1941-1945, representing the four years of labor in an ammunition factory during the war that my aunt had earned. They had prepared an album of pictures with a history of their family with English titles. I was embarrassed that my gifts to them were not as personalized as theirs.

Every chance I had, I stared at my aunt. Her face and facial expressions were so similar to my father's. I had the feeling that, even though he had died in 1963 and wasn't celebrating directly with us, indirectly he was observing our meeting and was deeply pleased.

We asked questions about their lives and they asked questions about ours. Gaps in personal histories were filled. I finally learned why my aunt had never left Russia. Her brother—my father—came first. Fifteen years later, his mother had come to live with us, but my aunt remained. Details of her life were fuzzy. She said prior to the war her husband had owned a chain of department stores. He sensed it was time to leave, and went to Brazil (where he had family) to establish himself in business. Just when he felt ready to bring his wife and son over, the Russian borders closed to emigration. Not wanting to leave them alone, he returned to Russia. His luck continued to be bad. He was drafted into the army and was killed shortly thereafter. She and her son, then fourteen, who had been left behind in Zaslav, were evacuated to the Ural Mountains just before the German army came. They spent four years making bullets in an ammunition factory for which the only pay was bread. The medal my aunt had given me was the one she had been given for her loyalty and service.

That night, sleeping on a very hard cot in our dumpy little hotel room, I dreamed I was walking past a window and there was my father smiling at me. He smiled at me—smiled the beautiful smile that I remembered from childhood. The smile told me how happy he was that his beloved daughter and his beloved sister were finally meeting.

We spent the next day—our last day—at my aunt's apartment visiting. After several hours, Semyon suggested we take a walk to the beach on the banks of the river. It was a warm, sunny day. As the seven of us marched down the street, he was so happy to have us there that he put his arms around our shoulders and broke into song. Every Yiddish song that we knew we sang together. The moment was spontaneous, incredible, and exhilarating. It was the perfect activity to share, since, other than that, we could only communicate through our translator.

Semyon pointed to the park ahead of us and, as we made our way to the edge of the water, we passed a pathetic array of rusted, broken playground equipment. When he told us the park was only eight years old, we were shocked. The boats at the river also looked very old and decrepit. We were shocked when he told us they were only five years old.

We spent the rest of the day pleasantly, everyone floating through this incredible fantasy together. We walked, talked, and just enjoyed sitting together. We listened eagerly to the army stories and details of everyday life there. Semyon's son, Leonid, had spent time at the Chinese border, but was now taking his wife and three-year-old daughter to Israel. He was extremely eager to leave as quickly as possible because he was deeply concerned that his child had some radiation sickness. She was quite pale and relatively listless.

His sister, Rita, who lived in Leningrad, told us that she spent an average of ten to twelve hours a week waiting in lines, but cheerfully added that it was no problem. She was used to it. It was part of everyday life. She was proud of her city, loved her work, and said she would never leave. (She is now living in Germany with her family.)

I realized that this generation was experiencing the same emigration problems of my aunt's generation. Some were leaving, some staying. And what I saw firsthand was the parents' and grandparents' feelings. Leonid's other grandmother, who lived with them, spoke of her upcoming loss. I began to understand what my parents—particularly my father—had experienced leaving his mother and sister behind. And what they felt when they let him go. These were parents wanting to give their children hope and a chance for a better life, but they knew that perhaps they might never see them again, certainly not as often. Leonid and his family did go to Israel, and Rita and her family moved to Germany. Eventually, Semyon and his wife, Bertha, joined them. No one stayed.

"How could they mismanage a whole country?" Sergei had kept repeating as we'd driven through the rich but untapped farmlands of Byelorussia on our way to Zaslav. He told us that when he had walked into an American supermarket for the first time, he cried and then thought, "I want my five-year-old son to buy tomatoes in a supermarket!"

My aunt's apartment, according to Sergei, was typical middle class Russian. They had nice rugs hanging on the walls and crystal and china in a cabinet against one wall. The interior of their home was well maintained, and they were proud of it. They loved their country, but were angry at the failure of the system.

Their cynicism was quite funny at times. In the car, whenever Sergei saw a policeman, he pulled the seatbelt in front of him and when the officer passed, he dropped it back.

"Sergei," I said, "What you are doing is endangering *your* life. You're fooling yourself, not the cop!"

He laughed, realizing I was right. "We're like little kids rebelling against our parents," he said. "In this country, you learn *not* to obey the law."

That three-day trip to Zhlobin was one of the most intense experiences of my life. When I said goodbye to my aunt, I tried to think of something I could say that would express what I had felt these past days.

"I have lost so many people in my life," I told her. "But now I have found one."

Amazing as this story is, what follows almost equals it. When we left Zaslav on our previous trip, I had the name and address of Frida Kirchik in Kiev. When I returned home I wrote to her. Again, I was intensely curious about this person. Could she be another long-lost relative? Soon, I received a three-page letter written in broken English signed by Frida Kirchik, but written by her daughter, Irina Kirchik. Sitting in my chair in my office in Bethesda, Maryland, I couldn't believe the words on the page. Irene Kerchek was my maiden name. How could this be? How could there be two people in the world with that unusual name?

With that first letter began a rapid back and forth correspondence between Irina and me. At first, we were just trying to establish how we were related. Neither of us had heard of the other, but with each letter we found more and more connections. The most important was a hotel that both our grandfathers owned in Zaslav and she had visited many times. We also shared a photo of my father's stepbrother, who was a concert violinist!

The speed of our correspondence had much to do with the fact that they were considering moving to the United States, and Abe and I were willing to help them. I knew they needed to work. I discovered that Irina was a master's degree musicologist and her husband, Leonid Entin, was a professional physical therapist. I hoped they would choose Washington rather than Chicago, where they had family as well. I went to work trying to see what we could do to help them find work. A musicologist? A physical therapist who couldn't speak English?

Loving challenges, I strained to think who needed someone with such high-level skills and experience in music. The physical therapist soon became a non-problem; he couldn't do that work without speaking to his clients. But, based on his army experience, we were able to get him a position as a chef.

As a knowledgeable Washingtonian, I remembered that the head of the Library of Congress, James Billington, was an expert on Russian music; in fact, he had an entire collection sitting in the basement of the library. Here was someone who could take it out of there. I convinced him that he couldn't put an ad in the paper and ever find anyone as qualified. It took some time to actually get her on board because of her foreign status, but she is still there to this day.

On our way home from Zhlobin, we stopped in Kiev and met the Entin family, two young parents with two young children. They were frightened. Leonid asked if we could take his gold coins with us, but we weren't willing to chance it. However, within a few months, they arrived in Washington with their children, Alina and Vlady. Today, Alina is a successful lawyer, married with two children. Vlady, also married, is a sponsorship salesman for the Washington Capitals. They live five minutes from me. Writing this memoir has brought together all these various experiences in a way that I had never anticipated. I found two families, an extraordinary find. Did it happen because I had lost so many? Probably. But it has been wonderful to learn more and more about people my parents left behind, but are in fact very much alive. Two Irene Kercheks?

CHAPTER SIX

A s lifelong, ardent Democrats, we were delighted when Bill Clinton was elected president and the party returned to power.

We were delighted on a personal level too, because, by that time, we knew the Clintons. I had been part of the group who had interviewed him (and then later backed him) when Pamela Harriman's "Democrats for the 80s" was deciding which candidate to support. Abe and I had contributed to his campaign and attended many of his speeches.

"How does it feel to be here?" I asked President Clinton one night when he had only been in office a couple of months and was giving us a tour around the White House.

"I still can't believe it," he said.

An ardent basketball fan, Bill Clinton came to a lot of games with us after he became president. Hillary came with him to a Chicago game, but he was the more constant fan. He credited his extensive knowledge of basketball to insomnia. He slept little, he explained, and watched just about all the games he could find on television.

Since Abe had always shunned the fancy "sky suites" we'd built at Capital Centre (which was renamed USAir Arena in 1993) because they were too far away from the action, we watched the games in the stands along with everyone else. No one enjoyed mixing with the other spectators more than Bill Clinton. This was the biggest "people person" I'd ever met. Sitting in the fourth row with us, he engaged anyone and everyone near him in conversation, teasing and joking and happily posing for pictures, and even volunteering to take pictures for those who asked him. He was a lot of fun.

One night when he came to the game, the Secret Service brought in a huge cardboard box, which they put on the floor in front of his seat. It was filled with soft drinks and snacks, and the next thing we knew, there was the President of the United States offering its contents to all the people sitting around him. Did he forget that he was the President of the United States? He was a natural politician.

Soon after they moved into the White House, we were invited to an informal dinner party that happened to be on my birthday. It was in a lower-level dining room with about five tables of eight people. I was seated at Bill's table. Toward the end of the meal, a birthday cake was brought in to my surprise, and everyone sang "Happy Birthday, Irene!" I was stunned and flattered. Was I really that important?

It was a welcomed moment after what had been a very low, emotional period for me. Earlier that year, Abe had done it again. In the seven years after our separation, and then subsequent reunion, we had gone back to normal in what felt like a very close marriage, going away just the two of us as he always requested on trips overseas and weekends at Cloverland.

Then suddenly, with no explanation, Abe once again just left home. I can't say it was a breakup. That term doesn't really describe it. It wasn't as if he was going some place else.

I wondered whether he was trying to leave me or leave his problems. He was the owner of two teams with more losses than wins; one team still losing millions of dollars annually. Wes Unseld was in his fifth year as head coach of the Bullets, and it was the team's fifth losing season in a row. No one adored Wes more than I did, but everyone— including me and Wes—was telling Abe it was time to find a new coach. But Abe was faithful to a fault and he wouldn't, couldn't do that. There were complaints about the high cost of parking at the USAir Arena, and the difficulty of getting there because of the lack of public transportation. Reporters were complaining that Abe was too cheap to spend the money to get good players who could win. Fans had begun yelling at him at games.

All this was very hard to take. For a man as intensely preoccupied with his public image as Abe was, this was very difficult. But why run away?

For the second time in our marriage, I had questions but no answers. This was a very affectionate husband (we always held hands as we walked), a thoughtful man who sent flowers on every possible occasion, who called me every day from the car announcing "This is your husband calling. I'll be home in twenty minutes." A man who on our last anniversary had written on the card: "Happy 48th! It is my hope and prayer we will go on to celebrate 49, 50, 51…All the way past 75!" And a man who, on Mother's Day, had written a poem to go along with the flowers:

> As mother and grandmother you have no peer,
>
> That's one reason I hold you so dear.
>
> But most important, as my wife,
>
> You're the essential person in my life.

Add to this the only explanation he'd ever offered for leaving me the last time— "I was unhappy." It was no wonder I had questions and no answers. I was shocked and clueless.

That did not stop the psychotherapist in me from speculating. Abe, I knew all too well by this time, had a burning, deep-seated need to be seen as the good guy, to be loved by all. He jumped at every opportunity where he could look good, whether it was delivering turkeys on Christmas, helping children through his work in UNICEF, or paying college tuition for those who couldn't afford it. These were more than public relations gimmicks. He wasn't pretending to be a good guy. He was a good guy. But it was a constant need to be seen as good, one that served the community but also served Abe himself.

However, a man who needs to be admired by the community, adored by employees, and still run a successful business needs people who handle the inevitable difficult parts. Abe, fortunately, always had people in his organization who happily took on the bad guy role. "I love firing people!" one senior executive told me one day at lunch.

I again went through a personal examination of my relationship with Abe. What role did I play for him? But these ruminations stopped after a while, along with the many questions that were never answered.

Abe returned home and I never learned the source of his "unhappiness." Perhaps, he never really knew himself. Like so many men, he never articulated his feelings. No matter, I still loved him with all his weaknesses. It turned out he had decided that the cure for his financial worries was not getting out of his marriage, but rather getting out of the USAir Arena. He was tired of all the complaints about the lack of public transportation and the congested parking lot. If he couldn't do anything about the team's records, he could build a new building. This was his forte. This he could control.

Some other franchises were building new downtown arenas. A state-of-the art facility could boost the value of the teams. Abe, typically thinking community, said, "Think of what it could do for the District of Columbia!"

This project was what he needed to renew his spirit. And mine. This was exactly the kind of activity that both of us had done with tremendous enjoyment over the years— finding a location, designing and building a new building. This was something he knew in his gut; nobody was better at this than him. We had built so many large buildings, each one more successful than the others. Getting it completed faster than anyone else was his specialty. We were back in our element.

Once the word was out that we were looking for a new site, several propositions came in from interested communities. Baltimore offered to build an arena down by the waterfront. There were possibilities in northern Virginia and in Columbia, Maryland. But, from the beginning, Abe wanted to be in downtown Washington, his hometown. He had tried unsuccessfully to negotiate something in the city before we built Capital Centre, and now the prospects looked better. The D.C. business community felt a downtown arena would be a huge boost to the city's commerce and was very receptive to the idea. The question was, where?

We looked at and rejected a number of sites. When Abe, our son, Robert, and I went to look at Gallery Place—then a mostly boarded-up plot of land between 6th and 7th Streets and F and G Streets downtown next to Chinatown—Robert opened the door to get out of the car and we said, "Wait! You can't walk around here." This was noon.

Everyone in Washington knew this area before the devastation. This was the fun area for shopping, starting at the old Hecht's at 7th and F and then walking up F Street to Garfinckel's Department Store on 14th Street.

Now this was burnt-out Washington. It had been part of the area torched in riots after the death of Martin Luther King, Jr. in 1968. Now, twenty-five years after those riots, it looked the same. "Depressing" was an understatement.

However, our advantage over other team owners was that we had been in the construction business. When we finally *did* get out of the car and start walking around, it was the possibilities we saw, not the boarded-up buildings. This plot of land was sitting on top of the Gallery Place Metro stop, which connected the red, green, and yellow subway lines, and it was just two blocks away from Metro Center, which linked the red, orange, and blue lines.

As we walked around and around, up 6th and down 7th Street, across F and G, we noted how close the location was to the National Portrait Gallery and the National Building Museum. We walked a few blocks down to Pennsylvania Avenue, and there in the distance, were the Mall and the National Gallery. The more we walked, the more we saw beyond the grit of the neighborhood and the more excited we became.

This was a great location. An arena could thrive in this neighborhood, and very possibly bring with it an economic revival.

The negotiations began. The first conflict was that Washington's business community was eager to have the arena built downtown, but the District government was heavily in debt and D.C. Mayor Sharon Pratt Kelly had little rapport with the business community.

One year before, when negotiations to build a new football stadium in the District had broken down, she had branded Redskins owner Jack Kent Cooke a "billionaire bully," forcing him to build a stadium near Capital Centre in Prince George's County.

Meanwhile, several groups in Maryland and Virginia were trying to persuade Abe to move there instead. Everyone seemed to want to build us an arena, but the District of Columbia.

Abe negotiated a deal with the District, and several people wanted to be part of it. Abe was never interested in partners, and always reminded me that I was his only partner. He was determined to build the "best new building in the country."

Abe's major concern was the District's finances. The city's debt kept climbing, from $500 million to more than $700 million. Abe worried that, even if the city agreed to finance the arena, it wouldn't be able to follow through.

By this time, Marion Barry had won the Democratic primary,

which meant he would soon be mayor. We had been friends with Marion for years, and Abe set up a meeting with him. Abe told Marion Barry that he would finance the arena himself if Marion gave him his personal word that he would run interference for him—that he would cut through the bureaucratic red tape the District of Columbia was known for and get things done quickly. Quickly was the operative word. This was more important to Abe than the money.

Marion gave his word. He did what he said he would do, creating a team to speed up all necessary permits, approvals and other paperwork, strategically warding off the opposition of preservationists when it became clear the building would slightly alter L'Enfant's design of the city, and sending the right lobbyists to Capitol Hill to convince Republican opponents this was a good idea.

According to the final deal, the District would contribute no money—just tax-free land and site preparation—and we would put up the money to build the arena.

"You realize we're putting just about everything we have on the line here," Abe warned me. I did realize it. It was scary, but I always had complete faith in Abe's business judgment.

From the beginning, Marion Barry asked the head of each city agency involved to work closely with the development team to fast track the project. He smoothed over relations with nearby Chinatown to make sure key elements of Chinese architecture were evident on the exterior of the building, from the pagoda-like gazebo and intricate latticework on the railings at the north entrance to elaborate brick murals inspired by the Chinese characters for longevity. This was a good sign!

On October 18, 1995, twenty-two years after the opening of Capital Centre, we picked up shovels and "broke ground" officially to build a beautiful new arena in what would become the heart of downtown Washington. And in a stretch of downtown Washington that had been a blight on the city for so many years. Things were good again in our house. This was again a project in which we could share and take pride together.

I was still working in my clinic, seeing patients, and writing papers about my Medical Crisis Counseling work. I was also serving on various health and mental health boards, including the board of the National Cancer Institute. At one of our meetings, one clinical trial received extra attention. As we sat around our huge conference table, one of our members commented quietly, "Why haven't there been any women included in this study?" This was not so unusual except for the subject of the study. We all took a closer look with this question in mind, and a major debate began about which studies should and should not include both sexes. The question now became whether women could still be added to this study or if it were too late. We even considered the possibility of tossing out the entire study. How many years and dollars had gone into this project?

As this critical discussion continued, a much larger issue emerged: women's health was not getting the same attention as men's. How could you include men and women in one study when the bodies were so different? Studies that had only used men as subjects were used to determine procedures and medications that were not applicable to women. It was as if a huge spotlight descended on that table, and we decided to throw out the study.

This was the beginning of a major shift in thinking about gender differences in medicine. Dr. Florence Haseltine at the National Institutes of Health, who had coined the term "sex-based biology" to refer to the study of sex differences in health and disease, was one of the leaders in this effort. Dr. Haseltine, Dr. Susan Blumenthal, and I helped organize the Society for Women's Health Research, which has grown to be the major organization in research and health promotion for women. I am proud to have been a part of this effort in women's health.

I attended one of the first luncheons in Washington to promote women's health, and that was the beginning of a new cause for me that continues to this day. After watching a CBS documentary to promote mammography screening as a means of preventing breast cancer, I spoke with a friend, Dr. Claudia Baquet, then the associate director of Cancer Control Science at the National Cancer Institute, about what we had just seen.

"African American women are the most difficult group to reach," Claudia said. "They have the lowest rate of mammogram testing."

Her comment struck a chord. African-American women?

"Claudia," I said. "I think I could do something about that."

"What?"

"Well, most basketball players' wives and girlfriends are African-American," I said. "And they tend to be celebrities in their communities. They easily can get publicity. They just have to say, 'I'm Wes Unseld's wife' and the cameras roll. These women could get a message out."

"Do you think you can do this?" Claudia asked.

I felt sure it would be a hit with the league as well as the women. I knew so many of them personally. The more we talked, the more excited I got about the idea. At home, even before taking off my coat, I went to the phone and called David Stern, the NBA Commissioner.

We were quite good and old friends. I blurted out my idea and he said, "Yes. I like it."

With my heart pounding, I called Dr. Sam Broder, the Director of the National Cancer Institute, explained my rationale, and that David Stern had approved. He said one word: "Brilliant!"

My next call was to Connie Unseld, Wes Unseld's wife, an old and dear friend. She was ecstatic. Now all we had to do was to organize it, something I love to do—especially when I had the NBA and the NCI behind me.

When I thought about how to engage the wives, I felt it was important for them to understand the issue of breast cancer and to actually see the National Cancer Institute, to meet the doctors doing the research, especially the women doctors. Then I felt they could go out in their communities and speak with authority.

With Connie, we contacted teams across the country and invited them to send two representatives to the National Institutes of Health for a one-day briefing. We arranged it so that they would not have to stay overnight, knowing that many of them had young children. Every team was enthusiastic and onboard.

We planned the day. We arranged for the women to meet the physicians, hear about their work, and ask questions. Next, they'd move into a wonderful, wood-paneled dining room with the flag of every team represented hanging from the ceiling.

The women were briefed by Dr. Bernadine Healy, who was the new head of NIH, as well as Dr. Vivian Pinn, the newly appointed head of the Office of Research on Women's Health. They also heard Senator Barbara Mikulski, a women's activist from my home state of Maryland. And, of course, my wonderful supportive husband, representing the NBA.

It was fabulous. Every NBA team sent one or two representatives, and we had buses pick them up at the airport. They listened to speakers, toured the institute, returned to their home cities, and began publicizing the need for mammograms. Each NBA team has a community outreach program, so all these women had to do was contact their own PR people and, boom, they were on television.

Connie named the program "NBA Wives Save Lives." It was a huge national success. (It's still going on after all these years.)

It was also a success on a personal level. I received a thank you note from an NBA coach, who said because of the program, his wife's cancer had been detected early enough to be cured. What gratification and what fun!

I moved on from this program to return to my clinical work and to write two books, but the experience opened the door to another area of women's health several years later—heart disease.

And, after a decade of blood, sweat, and tears, my manuscript on "overcoming the challenges of long-term illness" was finally finished! *Taking Charge* was intended for patients and family members as well as health professionals. Since my Medical Crisis Counseling model had been so successful in the clinic, I hoped to reach the needy audience with the written word. I knew my method and I had many patient stories. What I didn't have was the experience of writing a book. I had written many papers. How difficult would it be to put this familiar information into book form? All my false confidence came from members of my book club, most of whom were professional writers and editors. They knew of my work and assumed that I could do what they could do. Wrong!

Actually, it turned out to be two manuscripts. First published was *Taking Charge,* an anecdotal account of my patients and experiences using short-term therapy for dealing with chronic and terminal illnesses. And published one year later was *Medical Crisis Counseling,* which laid out my formula for short-term therapy.

What I learned from this ten-year odyssey was that I wrote these books in the wrong order. Had I written about my philosophy and methods first, it would have given me the outline I needed for *Taking Charge.* As it was, it took me ten years to complete the first book and only one to write the second!

Writing a book is an all-consuming task. Having a book published—that moment when you finally get the chance to hold the finished product in your hands—truly gives you a remarkable sense of accomplishment. It did for me. Now many people—patients, families, and health professionals—could potentially be helped by the methods I had developed and practiced for twenty-five years. The only downside was the shock to learn that television reporters, who were reporting on the book, rarely read it through. They assumed the books were about death and dying. In fact, they were about preserving the quality of life, planning a future, mastering fears! Another lesson learned.

Generally, life was good for Abe and me. We had a full life and mostly we were healthy and so were our children. Many of our friends were deeply involved in the media, the diplomatic world, and, of course, the sports world. We remained quite close with Yitzhak and Leah Rabin even after they left Washington and he became prime minister of Israel. We saw them whenever they visited Washington. We were not of the diplomatic world, so our friendship was just that, friendship.

In July 1994, they were in Washington and on a high. Yitzhak had just met with King Hussein of Jordan and President Clinton at the White House, where they had signed a document declaring an official end to the state of enmity that had existed between Israel and Jordan. The two countries would now begin negotiations, hopefully, that would lead to a lasting peace.

To celebrate this achievement, a few couples had lunch at the Four Seasons. I sat at the end of the table across from Yitzhak. I watched his glowing face as he described his meeting with King Hussein. I had known him now for years, and I had never seen him so effervescent. I couldn't help but say to him, "Yitzhak, I have never seen you this happy."

"And this is just the first step toward peace," he said, excitedly. "The next step will be signing a peace treaty between Jordan and Israel." As a parting gift, I gave him a small figurine of a juggler, symbolic of all that he was trying to accomplish. A few weeks later, I received a thank you note from Leah.

"That juggler sits at our bedside. And I look at him every day and think, 'How smart Abe and Irene were. What is Yitzhak if not a real juggler; struggling in all directions and seeing his targets in front of him and trying not to look right or left to get distracted."

On October 26, 1994, in a ceremony in the Arava Valley of

Israel near the Jordanian border, that is exactly what happened—the peace treaty was signed.

How can life's events take one from an incredible high to an incredible low in a flash? A year later, on November 4, 1995, Yitzhak was gone.

Our son, Jimmy, called us as soon as he heard the news that Yitzhak had been shot at a peace rally. We called our friend, his Chief of Staff, Amos Eiran. He reported that Yitzhak was in the operating room. There was still hope. But then our friend, newsman Herb Kaplow, who knew how close we were to Rabin, called to tell us he was dead.

The funeral was the next day. We chartered a plane with two other friends of the Rabins and flew there overnight. It was opening night for the Bullets—the only one we ever missed.

When we arrived, we had to make our way through the thousands of people standing outside the Rabins' apartment building lighting candles. Once inside, I sat down on the sofa next to Leah, we hugged as hard as we could. Neither of us are criers. There wasn't much to say. Just to be able to be there, sitting next to her and her children, was why we had made that overnight trip.

The next day at the funeral we sat behind President Clinton, who was very emotional, as was Teddy Kennedy, who, with tears streaming down his face, spread soil from JFK's grave over the coffin. When Jordan's King Hussein spoke at the funeral, saying he was "grieving the loss of a brother," I was reminded of the beautiful, animated expression on Yitzhak's face the day we had lunch in Washington as he spoke so excitedly about the possibilities that could come from his new relationship with the King of Jordan.

We were deeply touched by the experience and the loss. So much so that Abe decided to change the name of our team, the Washington Bullets. He had long been unhappy with the association of bullets and all the violence in Washington. We didn't give that name to the team. That was what it was when we purchased the team in 1964. Exploring the origin recently, I discovered it was named that because of a World War II ammunition factory, "faster than a speeding bullet!"

Yitzhak's assassination provided the impetus to rename the team. Abe announced a contest to choose a new name. There were many choices: Dragons, Express, Stallions, Sea Dogs, and Wizards.

The Wizards won. We were hopeful the name would bring some magic. Life soon became exciting and challenging—just the way that Abe and I seemed to function best. We were back in the building business, a business we both knew well and thrived on—the design, the deadlines, the completion of the building at each new phase. At least three times a week, every week for the twenty-five months it took to build it, Abe drove down to the construction site of the new arena—named the MCI Center (later changed to the Verizon Center)—rolled up his pants, pulled on construction boots, grabbed the hard hat with his name written across the back, and went to check on how things were going.

All did not go smoothly. The site turned out to be too small, so streets were closed and buildings torn down. There was the problem of contaminated soil, then a humongous snowstorm that slowed construction, then an asbestos problem, and then the "smart seats" turned out not to be that smart. I didn't literally go to the construction site, but knew every inch of the plans. Having the experience of Capital Centre behind me, I knew what we wanted in this building. The major innovation was the suites. In Capital Centre, we naively placed them in the top of the building (saving the better, lower seats for season ticket holders). Years later, we now understood this is not where people want to sit, especially when they are expecting luxury seating. This time, we had 110 suites, each one designed to hold about twelve people at two different levels, the lower one at eye level—only about twelve rows above the floor. Abe and I had a double suite with a private elevator that came right up from the garage. The major purpose of this feature was to provide privacy for any VIPs, including the President of the United States if he wished to visit, and accommodations for the Secret Service.

I also appreciated the fact that we could now create a beautiful building in downtown Washington. The MCI Center would be one million square feet and was designed to be as open to the city as possible, a place that was distinctly Washington, with lots of windows and sunlight beaming in on the concourses. On the south side you could see the Capitol dome. On the G Street side you could see the flag on top of the White House.

Inside it was designed to be a jazzy world of bright lights and vivid colors. There would be a sweeping concourse alive with commercial activity—food concessions, sports bar, restaurants, retail merchandising. Then there would be the breathtaking arena bowl with 20,000 purple seats and giant-screen, video cubes suspended from roof trusses longer than a football field. The rows of seats were designed to rise upward instead of sweeping back and away from the court. Even in the very top of the arena, spectators would feel much closer to the action than they had felt in lower seats at Capital Centre, by then known as USAir Arena. Abe and I both thrived on this kind of accomplishment, something you could see and touch.

On a cold night, December 2, 1997—a day before Abe's seventy-fourth birthday—the MCI Center became a reality. Opening night was just as glitzy as it could be. The arena debuted as a combination theater, night club, and sports center. Crowds cruised the concourse, checking out the food, and then climbed the glass staircase of the Velocity Grill, which had basketball-hide upholstery on the bar stools, shattered glass floor tiles, and hockey pucks on the walls.

Inside the arena, before the game, music poured from the speakers and laser beams spelled out the names and uniform numbers of the players. It was an amazing combination of sights and sounds. And to make the night perfect, the Wizards won, defeating the Seattle Supersonics—our old nemesis—95-78.

Naturally, there were many speeches. Everybody in the city of Washington wanted to be a part of this accomplishment. When it was my turn to speak, all I could think of at that moment was when I first arrived in Washington.

"Maybe someday we'll all be strolling up F Street again," I told them hopefully. "Up beautiful F Street!"

Sure enough, it had begun. As I watched all the people crowding the sidewalk outside after the game, I realized that for the first time in a long time, the square piece of land bounded by 6th and 7th, F and G Streets, was a place to be—not a place to flee!

I felt extremely lucky to have been a part of this project, of what Abe and I had put together and what the future held for the city.

CHAPTER SEVEN

Sometimes you arrive at your destiny in an indirect way. One of the most consistent problems I experienced in treating people with chronic illnesses was that so many would begin taking the drugs the doctor had prescribed, only to stop prematurely and without informing their physician. The reasons were often because they couldn't afford the cost, didn't wish to spend the money, were symptom-free, or felt the drugs had not made a difference.

I discovered this was a problem for more than my clientele; it was a trend. There was a critical need for drug companies to solve the problem of "noncompliance." There was a need to find ways to keep the patients on their prescribed drugs and for follow up. Since all of my patients were on some drug for their medical condition, I was quite familiar with this problem. Often my referring physicians turned to me for help.

Dr. Gerald Koocher, a psychologist at Harvard, and I created the idea of telephone counseling. We developed training—tapes, videos and other materials—to educate health professionals. Karen Christman, manager of the department of social work at Pittsburgh Children's Hospital, heard what we were doing and contacted me.

I went to Pittsburgh, and developed a training module. Soon after, we did two, daylong training sessions with the social workers who would be making the calls. We tried the concept in Pittsburgh, and it worked beautifully.

Feeling secure that we had a number of well-trained telephone counselors ready to go, Karen and I began visiting drug companies. We felt that they were the ones, as well as the patients, who'd benefit the most when patients adhere to the prescribed drug regimen. Many patients with a chronic illness, first prescribed a drug at age forty, could possibly be on it for the rest of their lives. The drug companies were definitely interested, but the timing for our product was off. Other psychology groups had developed other follow-up methods and sold them to the drug companies, but they were not successful. After reviewing some of their materials, I was not surprised. They usually consisted of a fairly detailed group of booklets with calendars the patients were supposed to fill out in detail, describing what prescriptions they were taking and when. How could this possibly work? If patients were too busy to take their meds, why would they sit down and tediously fill out detailed forms?

Sadly for us, the drug companies we visited had already invested in these complicated and impractical programs. They expressed interest in our program, but were reluctant to try anything new. We were not making any headway in getting funding when in an unexpected way, we found another interested party.

One evening, my husband and I were at a dinner hosted by Dan Snyder, a Washington businessman who was interested in buying the Wizards (he would later buy the Washington Redskins). I discovered that his business was health promotion and advertising. After discussing sports and basketball, Dan asked "What do you do, Irene?"

I gave him a brief overview of my clinical work and told him about our efforts to interest the drug companies in our compliance project.

He was intrigued and said his company could possibly help. At the time, he was running a successful advertising company working primarily with medical practices. I was immediately interested, and contacted the person he recommended at his company in Connecticut. A few days later, I explained the telephone-counseling program to several of his staff members. Rather than following my presentation, they drew my attention to another topic.

"Would you be interested in doing something with women and heart disease?" they asked. "Why?" I asked. The answer would set me off on a related, but different path, for the rest of my life.

"Did you know that heart disease is the number one killer of women?" Snyder's staffer asked.

"I did not know that," I told him. How could I not know that fact? I had patients with heart disease. I had done a video for the telephone-counseling program that included two women with heart disease. If I didn't know that, who did?

Why was he telling me this? He said that two companies—CVS and Pfizer—were interested in funding a women's heart disease awareness project. If I were interested, they would fund it. All I needed to do was to create the program.

All kinds of bells and whistles went off in my head. "Yes," I said. "I would be interested." In that extremely roundabout way, I began working on the issue of women's heart disease prevention. I like challenges. Abe and I were alike in that way. We were always looking for something new, something that no one else had ever done. What attracted me to this were the challenges and the possibilities. The challenges were finding ways to "get the word out"—to educate women about the disease. The possibilities were to be able to help prevent it. I learned that heart disease, this number one killer of women, was eminently preventable. In 85 percent of the cases, once you learned you were at risk, you could take specific steps to alter your living habits, diet, exercise, stress—and prevent it. I knew of no other chronic illness that could be prevented in so many instances. The fact there were so many ways to prevent the disease once you knew you were at risk made the cause very appealing to me. With two children born with severe congenital heart defects in which there was no way to avoid the outcome, I felt so strongly about having an option. If you're lucky enough to be born with a healthy heart, you should take care of it.

With the financial backing to move forward, the opportunity was extremely attractive. Telephone counseling would have to wait. I went home with a million ideas. One in particular began to gel: having a health fair where women could get free screenings. I believed that once a woman learned that she was at risk, the chances were high that she would take action and change her behavior.

Where would we do it? How would we do it? How would we spread the word? Most important, how could we attract women to come to these fairs, particularly working women? As I suspected, these women have little free time. Fortunately, I had a place for a health fair: the MCI Center. Considering my target audience—working women—downtown Washington was a perfect location. Washington's large number of government office buildings was filled with the women I wanted to attract.

"I don't understand why breast cancer gets all the attention?" Dr. Claude Lenfant, head of the National Heart and Lung Institute, asked when I met him in his office. "More women die of heart disease than breast cancer. Why don't they know?"

"Because breast cancer by definition singles out women," I said. "You have to separate women's heart disease from men's. It has to be heart disease for women! We need to put a spotlight on women and heart disease."

We began planning our first health fair around this basic premise. The immediate challenge was getting women to come to the event. We were, after all, targeting working women who were challenged by a lack of time for themselves. A small group sat on my porch for months, and we planned and planned. We targeted working women between the ages of twenty-five and forty-five because they were the ones who could benefit most by changing their lifestyle, and, if they made health changes, it could prevent having a heart attack within a few years. I also thought that if we could ask these women's employers to support healthy lifestyle changes, it would benefit everyone.

We began reaching out. We organized a council consisting of representatives from the business community, religious community, and local government, and met regularly in a conference room at the MCI Center.

To encourage employer support, we decided to have the health fair on a Friday morning rather than on a weekend. The idea was that the employer would support the employee by allowing her to miss one hour of work in the morning to attend to her heart health. On a Friday, the fair would not take her away from her family on the weekend. This was "her" time.

Fortunately, I had access to MCI Center's Head of Human Resources, Mary Davis. Not only did she help us understand how to reach out to both employee and employer, she helped us connect with businesses and government offices in Washington. By being able to reach these women through work helped to make the community aware of the risks of heart disease in women.

After almost a year of planning, we set up the fair on the concourse of MCI Center. During the year, we had courted various companies, large and small—anyone who wanted to reach women—to set up booths.

The excitement was building! Tommy Thompson, Secretary of Health and Human Services, was completely onboard and planned to attend, as well as local celebrities and a number of Congresswomen. For several weeks, we did television and radio promotion. I anticipated that women would not attend only to get screened, so I always emphasized the fun part of the event. My mantra was: "Come and have fun, and, while you're there, you can get screened." Even with all the planning, when the moment arrived, I didn't know whether hordes of women or no one would be waiting outside the door. On the opening day, February 16, 2001, Washington was hit with a major snowstorm. Knowing that Washington was a southern town, I was sure everyone would stay home. I was in the building at 7 a.m. When we opened our doors, 2,000 women where waiting outside in the snow. It was a huge success!

This was also the beginning of what would become "Sister to Sister," an organization dedicated to the prevention of heart disease in women. Another brief chance for me to deal with women-only presented itself in 1998, when the NBA Board of Governors approved the concept of a women's basketball league—the WNBA. We took the opportunity and created one of the first WNBA teams, the Mystics. We felt Washington could be a good city for a women's team because of all of the women working in downtown government offices. It would be easy to get to games at the MCI Center after work. And, as it turned out, it was. The Mystics' opening game at MCI Center brought in a league record crowd of 20,674. Included in that crowd was a stellar group of women I had invited to cheer them on: Tipper Gore, Supreme Court Justice Sandra Day O'Connor, Secretary of Health and Human Services Donna Shalala, and Maryland Senator Barbara Mikulski. It was a definite highlight for me to host this game and have the first chance to go into the locker room to congratulate the players like Abe always did. After thirty-plus years of having to wait outside as Abe went into the player's locker room, my time had come. We won that game. I rushed down to the locker room only to wonder what exactly Abe did when he walked into the players' locker room. Standing in front of these giant women athletes, anxiously awaiting the pearls of wisdom to come forth from the boss's mouth, I was completely at a loss. "Uh, good game!" and I was out of the door as quickly as I could run. I never went in again, though informally I did spend time with the staff and players. All of us enjoyed the camaraderie. It was also another chance for me to learn how to engage women.

Overall, team business was not good. The Capitals were still losing money, which meant that we were still losing money. By this time, we knew it wasn't the team's fault. For the first time in a quarter of century, the Capitals had reached the Stanley Cup Finals. It wasn't the fans' fault, either. The Capitals were playing to sellout crowds. It had to do with the business, which was dependent on television advertising. At that time, the large numbers of people who watched the other sports on television were not watching hockey.

Abe had considered selling the teams in the past, but he couldn't bear giving up what had been an important part of his life for so many years. Still, he thought, perhaps this might be a time to sell the Capitals, and then he could hold on to the rest of the businesses. He could offer the Capitals and, as an added incentive, a percentage—a stake —in the MCI Center and the Wizards.

This was a very difficult decision for Abe, but I strongly encouraged it. It would free him of some worries, but also keep him involved. Even more important, he could still maintain control of everything else. Control was essential to Abe.

And so, the bidding began. Abe set certain criteria. He wanted to sell to someone local. It was very important to him that the teams he had brought to Washington stay in Washington. He wanted payment in cash because that would lessen the debt he'd taken on while building the MCI Center and enable him to continue his philanthropic activities.

From the beginning, Ted Leonsis, an AOL executive who had made a fortune from the company's soaring stock, was in the bidding. The problem was he wanted to buy everything, and that was not a possibility. Still, after he met with Abe and our son, Robert, early on, Robert stayed in touch with him by e-mail and a relationship developed between the two of them.

Variables began popping up. Buyers wanted to buy the Capitals and a share in the overall operations. In one instance, upon Abe's death, they could buy the rest. I scotched that offer myself.

The night before we were supposed to sign with three potential buyers, Abe was sitting down the hall from my bedroom in my office talking to one on the phone with the door open when I heard him say something that caught my immediate attention. What I thought I heard was something to the effect that rather than waiting for Abe to die, if he just became quite ill, and was lying in a hospital bed, he would have to sign off on the deal.

Running down the hall, I screamed at Abe, "What? Is that true?" And when he nodded, "Yes." I said, "I will never sign anything like that!" I imagined Abe lying dying in a hospital bed and the men waiting for the moment when we both would sign. That stopped that negotiation—and brought an unpleasant end to our relationship with those buyers. But those acrimonious negotiations made Ted Leonsis' group look very good. He was local. He was an avid sports fan. He had the money. He was willing to settle for the right of first refusal—an agreement that we couldn't sell the enterprise to anyone else without first giving him the chance to negotiate a deal.

And so the decision was made: We sold the Capitals and 19 percent of the umbrella company for our other holdings (the Wizards and MCI Center) to a group headed by Ted Leonsis. It was a very hard decision for Abe, and I knew it, but it also relieved him of a financial burden.

The decision was eased somewhat by the fact it brought little immediate change in our lives. Our life still centered around the MCI Center, soon renamed Verizon Center. Our suite there became almost our second living room. It was in an enormous complex. To enter the center, we had to drive up to the side of the building where, once the staff spied us, (Their code names for Abe and me were Verizon One and Verizon Two) huge, metal rolling gates rolled up slowly. From there, we rode down a steep ramp and into the enormous underbelly of the building. Driving past an area filled with travel buses, media trailers, stacks of tables, goalie cages, basketball hoop stands, and other large equipment, I always wondered how they could find anything in this vast storage area. And then there were usually groups of kids practicing for their brief appearances during halftime. Entering the building like this always filled me with growing excitement. Even though I knew what event I was coming to see, I did not know how it would end.

Once inside, we were always greeted warmly by the employees, "Hi, Mr. and Mrs. Pollin!" So many of them had been working for us for 30 years or more since Capital Centre had opened. We knew so many of their names, and in many cases, we knew their families.

Parking as close as we could (between more equipment) to the entrance to the arena floor, we walked down the long corridor past the locker rooms for the Wizards, Capitals and visitors to an elevator that went directly into our suite. This was pretty elegant given that we had always sat in regular seats at Cap Centre. We had moved up in the world.

I had designed the suite to be a welcoming place. It was twice the size of the average suite so it could accommodate our private guests, but also potential season ticket holders and sponsors. I wanted it to be elegant but simple. I used blond, wooden furniture and light fabrics with lots of overhead lighting. A large round table served as a buffet, and there was a long marble counter with bar seats facing the playing area. Just below that level, were two rows of leather seating for guests.

Over the years, we had many friends who joined us, usually major sports fans. So much so that some were "regulars." Here there were no political discussions. Republicans and Democrats came and left work behind. They all shared the excitement of the game. Occasionally, as is typical in Washington, some non-sports fans came to do "business." They would stand around the buffet table, drinking and schmoozing during the game, which really upset Abe. He always focused on the game and wanted everyone else to do the same. He would often make a face, and that would take care of it.

We had many regulars, friends who were as passionate as we were. Columnist Charles Krauthammer used to come quite often, even though we didn't agree on our political views. President Clinton was also a regular. He told me he watched repeats of Wizards games when he couldn't sleep.

I loved watching Bill Clinton work the suite. He was such a natural politician. Always, as he entered the room, his eyes would scan the group. He seemed to be making a mental note of everyone. Unlike the guy at the cocktail party who is looking over your shoulder to see if there is someone more important behind you he might talk to, his goal was to be inclusive. It didn't matter whether they were men or women, celebrities, bartenders, or waitresses, Bill Clinton always seemed to feel he had to make contact with every person in the room. If they didn't go over to him, he would eventually get to them. I think it was instinct with him. It was as though he needed constant reaffirmation and he did get it.

At halftime, Abe and I always walked around the suite, mingling with the guests, getting a snack from the buffet table. One night when Bill Clinton was there, I decided to see how important it was to him to mingle, to make contact with everyone. I decided to stay as far away from him as I could outside of his sight line and see if he would eventually make it to me. Did he really need to see and touch everyone in the room?

Watching him, I could see him greeting, talking, working his way from one person to another, and finally making his way to me—the person farthest from him. He did what I had expected. As usual, President Clinton had charmed every person in the suite, including his hostess.

All the years of experience in the building business gave us a sense of what buildings could do for neighborhoods. We knew that building the MCI Center in that part of downtown Washington could eventually turn a downtrodden area into a thriving commercial area. That has been our intent. We always said, "It's going to change the neighborhood," but we also thought it would happen sometime in the future. We weren't naïve enough to believe that the MCI Center was going to change things immediately.

But, that's practically what happened. The boarded-up neighborhood transformed itself almost overnight. The rundown little place where Abe and I would go for soup and a sandwich across the street was replaced by an upscale bistro. There were restaurants, condominiums, a movie complex, and even the Spy Museum, making the 7th Street corridor D.C.'s very own Times Square.

We could have profited enormously by investing in that area. While the center was under construction, Abe was offered neighboring properties for very little money. We could have bought the whole area! But Abe was, as always, extremely vigilant about his reputation. He didn't want to be thought of as "money greedy." He turned down all the offers. I was very proud of this attitude, and agreed with it completely. We didn't build the MCI Center to make a killing. In fact, you don't go into sports and make a killing. We didn't want to lose money either. The best situation was keeping the operation at top level, have winning teams, provide great entertainment, and serve the community. A balance to be sought, but not always achieved.

Needing to keep that balance was the reason Michael Jordan came to our team in 2000. Teams and fans were not happy. They needed a boost. Having him in Washington would definitely do it, and it did. The MCI Center came alive when Michael Jordan retired from the Chicago Bulls and joined the Wizards' front office as President of Basketball Operations and a part owner. Ted Leonsis had made the first contact with Jordan, and Abe thought it was a great idea. He was thrilled to have Michael Jordan. He had always respected him as a player, even though in 1998, fractious labor negotiations between the owners and the players caused an open shouting match between them.

"You should sell your team if you can't afford to run a franchise," Michael had yelled at Abe.

"Who are you to tell me to sell my team? It's my team and I'll do what I want with it." Abe had yelled back.

There was no talk of that history when Michael came to our house for dinner. Over poached salmon (which Michael said he'd never had before, being more of a steak and ribs guy himself) and lots of basketball stories, Abe and Michael definitely got past any negative feelings about each other. We had a wonderful time. I showed Michael the picture I had—still, after so many years—of him posing with our thrilled little granddaughters, Emma and Hannah, when we'd gone to the Bulls game in Chicago a few years earlier to celebrate an anniversary.

Michael was a charmer, somewhat like Bill Clinton in his energy and outgoing personality. We'd kept the get-together a secret because we worried if the neighbors knew, there would be a crowd outside our front door. Michael had arranged to be surreptitiously dropped off and later picked up. When the pick-up was late in returning for him, he looked at his watch and jokingly asked if we had a bed long enough, just in case. His ride did eventually arrive.

Abe gave Michael legal authority to do anything he wanted with the team, and Michael made it clear he was going to do something big. "My imprint, my footprint, will soon be all over this franchise," he told the press. We were ready for him to bring his magic with him.

I particularly enjoyed his company—at training camp, in our suite at games. I would visit him in his office and sometimes we'd chat on the cellphone. When we'd walk out of the building together, hundreds of adoring children followed us. I had known a lot of famous basketball players over the years, but he was definitely the "super, superstar."

We were good friends, and his mother was active in my Sister to Sister health fairs in Chicago.

Since our first heart health fair had been so successful, everyone, including our sponsors, Pfizer and CVS, wanted to try it again. The following year, we did it again at the MCI Center, and twice the number of women attended. Four thousand came to get their blood pressure, cholesterol, and blood glucose levels checked. For those who received results that were not in the range considered acceptable, we had counselors on hand to offer advice on how to begin to make changes—everything from modifying their diet to increasing physical activity, stopping smoking, and reducing stress. I put a particular emphasis on the reduction of stress wherever possible, recognizing the amount of stress in the lives of young working women.For our third Sister to Sister health fair, we partnered with the American Heart Association, which enabled us to expand to three additional cities: New York, Chicago, and Philadelphia. And we also added a new employee, a robot we named Holly Heart.

One beautiful summer day in Washington, Abe and I attended a street festival sponsored by the Wizards. The star of the festival was a robot that began talking to us. Yes, talking to us! To our delight, it had us laughing! It had the most amazing personality. It could talk and even respond to what was said. It would answer all our questions. I was so taken with this robot that when I arrived home I called Ray Raymond, the man who had created it, and asked if he could create a woman robot, one we could use at our health fairs. When he said he could, I was thrilled with all the possibilities. She could become our "spokes robot."

Working on this together for several months, we developed her personality. What did she need to be like to talk about women and heart disease to the public? My response was that she should be funny and quick, as well as knowledgeable about the relevant information about heart disease. She should also be cute and even a little flirtatious. She was to be about 5'2", very feminine, and pretty.

After several months, Ray Raymond created her with a very sexy voice. She attended not only all our health fairs in Washington, but also became the center of attention. She was invited to appear on the *Today Show*. She was so flirtatious that when she asked Al Roker if he wanted to touch her heart, he became embarrassed and couldn't answer.

This flirty quality almost got her into trouble on Capitol Hill. We'd done a presentation, and she sidled up to Senator Arlen Specter from Pennsylvania and asked, "Can I come home with you?"

Speechless, he said, "Well, um, I'll have to ask my wife."

She was also extremely competent. One day I took Holly to a scientific meeting at NIH with some of the top women in the health field. I told them to ask any question of her and amazingly she answered them. They couldn't believe it! How he programmed her so brilliantly, I'll never know.

To add to the fun and her ability to answer serious questions, we developed a song for her. I wanted the lyrics to state the essence of what we were doing in Sister to Sister. Fortunately, I had a wonderful friend who was a "music man." He had written many lyrics for advertising and knew exactly what I wanted. Bill Backer and I put a song together for her. The title: "If I Only had a Heart." It had a lot of meaning for me because it represented what my children, Linda and Jay Jay, didn't have. If they had been born with a healthy heart, they would have had the opportunity to take care of it. The theme of the song was "If I only had a heart, here's what I would do to take care of it." It became her signature at all of our health fairs. The message to the participants was just that: if you are lucky enough to be born with a healthy heart, you have the chance to take care of it.

While my health fairs were expanding all over the country, the Wizards did not improve under Michael Jordan. It was proving to be frustrating and embarrassing for him and us, the owners, given all the grandiose predictions, like the team would be at least at the .500 mark within a year or two. Sports writers were beginning to go after him for not delivering as promised, then for not "being on the job." They were reporting that he was "phoning in" his responsibilities, spending only about ten days of every month in D.C. They said Nike commercials, football games, gambling in the Bahamas, and playing golf were taking precedence over the Wizards. Michael's response was that he was about "winning, success, work ethic, giving everything I have." Finally, responding to public pressure, he said he would come back and play himself. This was a grand gesture, but would it work?

Abe and Ted found this idea appealing. They knew the tremendous fan and media support he had. It would certainly make things very exciting. It was agreed that Michael would return to uniform for a year or two. It was a quick fix. We knew that Michael would fill the stands and create frenzy among fans, which could only be good for the team. And indeed he did.

By thirty-eight, players are considered over the hill. But Michael Jordan over the hill was still an amazing spectacle to watch. Although plagued by injuries, he still led the team in points scored, and made history as the first forty-year-old to tally forty-three points in an NBA game. However, as a player, he wasn't good for the team in other ways. When the team failed to improve, he drove the players hard, creating dissension. The coach he hired alienated many of the players, benching them for long periods of time. Young players were coming to Abe to complain. What at first glance had appeared to be an inspiring solution slowly began to disintegrate. At the end of the season, Michael began admitting he'd made mistakes, but felt that he had grown as a manager and was now committed to coming back the following year and improving the team. He met with Abe to renegotiate his contract. He wanted to return as President of Basketball Operations, which would give him say on final draft choices, hirings and firings, and the formation of the roster. This would give him more control, but given his history—failing to make the playoffs, friction between him and some of the players and the coach he hired—there was a lot of skepticism among the owners. His new hires had raised questions about his abilities as a talent evaluator, and there were the questions of how much time he was spending on the job.

After many carefully thought-out meetings with senior staff and lawyers, Abe agreed to meet with Michael in his office. Knowing this would be a difficult meeting, his advisers suggested he tell Michael that "he had decided to go in a different direction." They felt, after reviewing his performance, they had no choice. It was not personal. They all liked and admired Michael; it was purely business.

This was not what Michael expected. He was shocked. What followed was a heated discussion of what had and had not been promised. But after Abe repeated his decision "to go in a different direction," Michael lost it. He became very angry and began shouting. At that point, Abe walked out of the room as Michael called him several unflattering names. Michael stormed out of the room, went down to the parking garage, jumped into his Mercedes convertible with Illinois license plates, took the top down, and drove directly back to Chicago.

Abe came home extremely shaken. In fact, I had never seen him so upset over team business. He never expected such a reaction. He'd always been a good negotiator. People always responded to him positively in those situations because he was "cool" and fair. This had never happened to him. It probably was a first for Michael as well. Nobody had probably said no to him in a long time.

During the following week, while we were taking a few days in Rehoboth, Abe was still visibly upset. As one of Michael

Jordan's biggest fans, I had a difficult time coming to terms with this situation. Life in professional sports can be extremely harsh at times; by now I understood this. What happened? I could say a breakdown in communications, but there were too many threads to tease out.

As with what happened with Michael Jordan, unfulfilled expectations also happened in my experience with Sister to Sister and the women's heart health projects. Based on our unbelievable success with our health fairs, now in four cities, our year-long relationship with the American Heart Association was beginning to fray. The health fair model, which had worked so successfully for us, was not the Association's style. It's a huge organization; we were small and flexible. Where we were willing to become an addition to their activities, they saw us as competitors. I believe we would have expanded their already successful organization into more one-on-one activities, but they could not change what had been their business model for years. Basically, our style of operating was too different from theirs and the relationship just wasn't going to work. I had hoped we would find a way of working together, complementing each other, but after one very long meeting, my board members and I decided to go it alone. Yes, it was scary, but we had good support. And I already knew what had been successful with three years of health fairs. We did continue, and continued to grow from four cities to twenty. We screened more than 100,000 women from varied economic, ethnic, and religious backgrounds. We learned what women would and would not respond to. We definitely made an impact. The next challenge was to have them follow through.

Writing this book has made me realize how many times both Abe and I had risen to challenges. It was obviously something we both loved and thrived on. Again, totally out of the blue, one evening the phone rang. In addition to telling me what time he would be home for dinner, Abe told me, "We just bought a synagogue."

"You what?"

"We just bought us a synagogue."

"What are we going to do with a synagogue?"

An hour later, at dinner, he explained.

Earlier that day he had received a call from a Washington builder telling him that one of the oldest synagogues in town, located up the street from the MCI Center, was about to be sold the next day and turned into a night club. Although we had never been members, we were familiar with the building. It was a beautiful synagogue. When the membership had moved to the suburbs, it had fortunately been sold to a black church. Now the church's membership had moved and they needed to sell. Fortunately, the synagogue was well maintained. We were one of three families who wanted to purchase it together, and we were all dedicated to saving it. We had no idea of what we would do with it except to simply save it.

The first task was to restore the building to its original beauty. It had become a major community resource. At first, no one realized the need for such a resource in that part of the city. It was a place where young people working in downtown Washington could come and meet, and a venue for everything from lectures, concerts and performances to weddings and other celebrations. It incidentally also became a place where many of the young people could find potential partners. The current problem was how to plan for the future, and other cities around the country were eager to learn from the success. Abe and I were extremely proud to be a part of this wonderful addition to the city.

The year 2005 was good for the Wizards. We made it to the playoffs. It was the second time the team had done so since 1979, and no one was more ecstatic than we were. We'd been team owners now for more than forty years, and we were still experiencing incredible lows every time the team lost, and insurmountable highs when they won. You'd think by now we'd been through enough victories and defeats to take them in stride, but we never did. Our mood was directly dependent on the team's proficiency. This was a big winning year with Larry Hughes, Gilbert Arenas, and Antawn Jamison working together brilliantly to help pull it off. We were feeling very upbeat.

Every cloud has a silver lining, but every silver lining also has a cloud. Abe's back had been bothering him for a while, a vestige of the old injury he'd sustained as a teenager working on his father's construction job. Somehow he had lived with it all these years, but now it was becoming more debilitating. For the first time, he considered surgery. We visited a number of surgeons, and finally decided to go ahead, but to do it before the season began again in the fall.

Being cautious, Abe had his heart checked to make sure that he could withstand the procedure. He decided to go to the Cleveland Clinic where he had had his successful bypass twenty-five years earlier. Although there were no signs that anything was wrong with his heart, it would be wise to go there for the consult.

The plan was to have a consultation in the early afternoon and head home that evening. He was in a good mood. He had completed successful negotiations for the Wizards. When we walked into the doctor's examining room, the first thing the doctor said was "Mr. Pollin, you look great!" He did. We spent two hours reviewing Abe's current physical status. The doctor said, "Mr. Pollin, you should do fine in surgery but it would be a good idea to have an angiogram." There was no sense of urgency; it was said only as a precaution. Abe wanted to get this surgery out of the way as quickly as possible. He jumped out of his chair, began to remove his jacket, and said, "Let's do it now!"

We were just supposed to do a quick consult and go home. Since there was no urgency, I suggested that we have it done in Washington. He was adamant. The doctor wanted to please him, and left the room to check out the schedule. He returned and said he couldn't do it then, but possibly early the next morning. Abe put his jacket back on and told the doctor we would be there early the following morning. We checked into the hotel next door and had a pleasant dinner in the dining room. Hopefully, we would still be home later the next afternoon.

We arrived in the hospital at five the next morning. The waiting room was already filled with people. We sat down, and soon the doctor appeared and got Abe. He said the procedure would take about a half hour. I pulled out one of the books I had with me and began reading. As promised, after a half hour, the doctor returned. "We did the angiogram," he told me, "but we found some blockage. It looks like we're going to have to put in a stent." This did not frighten me because stents had become rather routine.

Asking the doctor how long this procedure would take, he said, "About a half hour."

He walked away. I felt assured, and went back to my book. But it wasn't a half hour. Gradually, the waiting room began clearing out. An hour passed, and another. I didn't want to panic, but needed to know what was going on. I asked the woman at the receiving desk if she had any more information. She didn't.

More hours passed. The waiting room had emptied and still no doctor. By this time, I was in a state of panic. I was now the only person in the waiting room. My heart was pounding. Why was no one telling me anything? Where was Abe? What were they doing in there?

The doctor finally appeared. He walked to me in the waiting room and suggested we go into a room to talk. I was barely controlling the shaking of my entire body. Having taken patients and family members into these rooms myself, I knew what this room was about. This is it. This is serious. Something terrible has happened.

I was right. "Your husband has had a major heart attack," he told me as calmly as he could. "He might have had a stroke too."

Sitting across from me, with a pad in his hand, he began drawing diagrams and pictures—explaining that because Abe's artery was twisted, they couldn't get the stent in quickly. They kept trying and trying. The trying, he said, had caused the heart attack. I was sitting there facing him, looking at the diagram but not seeing anything. I was barely able to blurt, "Where is Abe?" I asked. "I want to see Abe."

Walking me back to the intensive care unit, I was surprised to see Abe looking as well as he did. Abe seemed himself. He was perfectly lucid and fairly strong.

Jimmy, Robert, Sigrid, and Hannah all arrived the next day, and as we stood around his bed, he was kidding around with everyone. His color was good. This was amazing given his diagnosis. We all felt a sense of relief.

While we were standing around Abe's bed, a team of doctors came in for their standard rounds. Several of them explained what had happened to Abe. The one woman doctor in the group disagreed. They attempted to override her, but I had the feeling we were not being given the whole story. Within a few days, we would know it.

Several days passed. Abe's condition worsened to the point that we had to get a special nurse to lift him. He had become as limp as a rag doll. This was the same man who, only three days before, had marched into the doctor's office in good health. Now he could barely lift his body. It was a dramatic turnaround.

Our focus was not on the cause of the heart attack, but what could be done. We were all in shock. How could I get my husband back? Would there be any surgery available? What could they do to save my husband's life?

This was the Cleveland Clinic, the best heart hospital in the world. After much consultation, we were told that there was a possible heart bypass surgery available, but the question was whether he was strong enough to survive it. He was getting weaker by the minute. How sick was he?

One day, the surgeon suggested a consultation in his office with the children and me. With the five of us facing him behind his desk, he asked if we were willing to deal with the results of the surgery. Not understanding, we asked for more details. As gently as he could, he explained that Abe could come through the surgery, but would never be the same vigorous man that he always was. Were we willing to accept that reality and live with it? We did not fully comprehend what this could mean, but we wanted our Abe to come through, no matter in what condition. We accepted.

Next, the kidney specialist said that Abe's kidneys were in such bad shape that he refused to join the operating team until they had improved. "I don't want to be there when he dies on the table."

This controversy between the doctors went on for five weeks, during which time the kidney surgeon went on a two-week vacation. I remained in Cleveland, but my children and other family members were flying back and forth. The kidney surgeon was adamant; Abe had to be ready.

Finally, a decision was made to go ahead. The kidney surgeon agreed and the team was ready. The heart surgeon's specialty, we were told was the "re-do." That meant someone like Abe who had had a previous bypass. The only question that remained was if the family was willing to accept the condition that Abe might be in after the procedure. He needed to feel the family support before proceeding. "I wouldn't be doing this if the family support isn't there," he told my children and me. "Are you sure you want to go through with it?"

Looking at him, we replied with one voice, "Yes, we want to do it."

What was the choice? No matter what lay ahead, we were willing to deal with it.

The surgery was successful, meaning that miraculously Abe survived. With modern technology, the medical profession can almost get the sickest person through surgery and declare it successful. Abe was then placed in an intensive care unit with tubes coming out of just about every part of his body. But he was alive! And starting his recuperation.

All this was taking place during basketball trading season. This being Cleveland, one morning as I approached Abe's bed, I saw the top news item on the TV was Wizards player Larry Hughes announcing he had just signed on with the Cleveland Cavaliers for $70 million over five years.

Standing next to Abe, with tubes coming out of every possible orifice, I was hoping that he hadn't seen or heard it. I quickly turned off the set. Abe was just beginning to recover, barely alive. How would he react if he discovered that Larry Hughes had not kept his promise to him?

"Keep the television set off," I instructed the nurses as I left the unit.

For the moment, I had prevented Abe from learning this stunning and disappointing news. Eventually, he did learn what Larry had done. By that time, he had accepted it. More than forty years in professional sports had taught him to deal with crisis like this. It would pass. Other events in our lives were more important.

The next day, as I walked into the intensive unit at my usual time, there was my husband, still held down with multiple wires and tubes, unable to speak but smiling broadly. Sitting in front of his bed, on top of a high rolling cart, was a huge round birthday cake. The shiny white icing was almost blinding and bright red strawberries completely covered the top.

He was grinning from ear to ear. I knew he could not respond, but I asked anyway how he had arranged the cake. He pointed to the nurses standing near the bed. I had forgotten it was my birthday, but he hadn't.

When he came home from Cleveland, he was still very weak. According to a physical therapist who came to see him soon after we arrived home, the weakness was from the heart attack. The contrast was stunning between the day we went for a consult to Cleveland to determine if Abe was healthy enough to undergo back surgery and five weeks later. The recovery was slow, but I hoped he could recover at the beach as he did after his bypass. I again rented a house in Jamaica.

A few hours after our arrival with our son Jimmy, Abe began to swell. Calling in a local physician, the doctor suggested we return home immediately. Abe was never to be the same.

At home, with physical therapy and a great effort on his part, he got to the point where he could drive his car and go to the office. He would never, however, return to the healthy state he'd been in the day we walked into the doctor's office and the doctor said, "Mr. Pollin, you look great!" Life went back to normal, at least temporarily.

I continued my work with Sister to Sister. We received an enormous boost from First Lady Laura Bush when her secretary called me at home one evening and asked if she could attend our next health fair. Laura Bush was calling us? She wanted to do something to help prevent women's heart disease. She loved what we were doing and asked if she could attend. Not only did she attend, she was an absolute delight, a very classy First Lady. She was warm, relaxed, and engaging as she walked around the concourse, greeting all of the delighted women who attended. Unlike so many of the First Ladies who view such events as photo ops and leave quickly, Laura sat down with one of the counselors and interviewed her. She became seriously interested in the cause, so interested that she became involved on her own, holding several receptions in the White House. The fact that I was a Democrat never stopped her from joining us in our efforts to help women prevent heart disease.

By this time, we had screened more than 50,000 women for heart disease early warning signs. We were on a roll, extremely pleased with the progress we were making.

One day, the sky began to fall. Abe, on his usual call from his car on his way home from the office, told me that he had to pull off the road. His eyelids were closing.

"What?" I asked, "You're saying your eyes are closing involuntarily without you wanting them to?"

"Are you tired? Sleepy?"

"No," he said. "I just can't control them. They are just closing."

That is exactly what they were doing. This became a pattern for a number of months, strange because there didn't seem to be any particular time or cause for it to occur. It would just happen.

This could be an early symptom, but of what?

We would be having a quiet dinner at home when suddenly his eyelids would close. It was extremely frightening for him and for me looking at this happening without knowing why.

A few months later, as we were leaving the White House Correspondent's dinner at the Willard Hotel in downtown Washington, a strange thing happened. I was walking down the steps and I heard a soft thud from just behind me. Abe had just plopped down on the steps. Without any warning, his legs just gave way. I helped him up, but he seemed confused. He had no control over his legs.

As weeks passed more strange falls happened. He'd just go down without any warning. He'd drop down in the shower, even on the carpet in our bedroom, and then be unable to get up on his own. He wasn't able to figure out how to get up once he was down. How could this be? This was a very well-coordinated, former athlete who couldn't raise himself up? Doctors came up with various diagnoses, such as Parkinson's disease, but he didn't have all the typical symptoms. Another doctor diagnosed it as PSP—progressive supranuclear palsy—a rare brain disorder that causes progressive problems with balance, eye movement, and thinking. But Abe had no trouble thinking and eye movement was not his problem; his eyelids drooped and his legs gave away.

Time was passing. With each day, he was losing normal movement. We had to retain a nurse to help him manage the stairs. And soon his neck needed support to hold up his head. Then each hand become useless and he was no longer able to control his foot movements. No doctor had yet been able to find the cause of this increasingly severe handicapping condition. The progression was relentless. He could no longer climb the stairs, then he could no longer walk, then he could no longer hold a fork in one hand, and then the other.

Little by little, Abe was losing ability to move on his own. He was now in another bedroom in a hospital bed with nurses around the clock. We put an elevator chair on our staircase. We did not know what to do next, but we did know that it would only worsen.

This increasingly growing physical inability occurred over the course of two years. During this extremely difficult time, I never left him. Just as I stayed with him at the Cleveland Clinic for five weeks, I would stay with him for however long it took.

I never considered it a burden, because that is where I wanted to be. I preferred sitting with him watching "I Love Lucy" than being anywhere else. His mind remained absolutely clear to the very end. He never lost his cognitive ability or his sense of humor. We had been together our entire lives. We were each a part of the other. If he was home, that is where I wanted to be.

It helped that his personality never changed. We could still hold hands and we could still argue. He remained the same control freak he had always been—enjoying the same "good guy" reputation he had so carefully developed over the years with me as his perfect foil. But I always knew his need to be the "good guy."

Yes, there were difficult situations, but humor always helped us to deal with them. One evening I decided to test whether we could still do this. I sat down across from him as he was sitting in his lounge chair, and keeping a straight face, said, "You want to control the nurses because…"

"Yes," he said, "I want to control the nurses because…" with his straight face.

I tried again. "You want to control the nurses because…"

With no hesitation, "I want to control the nurses, because."

Knowing I had lost again and fighting my desire to begin laughing, we both burst out laughing and that was the end of that exchange. I was grateful for that aspect of his personality.

We were still able to go to games in a special van that accommodated his wheelchair. The staff at the Verizon Center—the new name of the MCI Center—was amazing. When Abe could no longer feed himself, one of the big security guys would sit down and feed him. The usher in our suite always maneuvered his wheelchair close enough to my seat so that we could hold hands. Neither one of us had ever asked him to do that.

Throughout, Abe was determined to live life as much as he could with whatever he had, and I was determined to help him do so. His courage was remarkable.

Given that stubborn determination, we were still able to make it up to Tanglewood Music Center near our house in the Berkshires, even though he couldn't sit or hold his head up.

Another trip was to Wizards' training camp in Virginia just two months before he died. I knew how much he wanted to go. We had been going every year. The challenge was how to get him there?

At this point, he couldn't get in or out of an airplane. I was determined. I found a company that specialized in completely outfitted buses often used for political campaigns. They had beds as well as a full kitchen. On the first day of the training camp, my son, Jimmy, and I climbed into this bus with Abe and drove for several hours to the camp. Abe seemed completely content watching the football game on the television set over the bed.

Arriving at the building, we went onto the basketball court where the staff and players were amazed and pleased to see Abe.

Each one came over to hug him and me. Abe was extremely happy that we had made that trip. Basketball had been a part of his life for over forty years. And mine.

Having worked professionally with many neurological patients over the years, what terrified me the most was the possibility that Abe would lose his ability to speak to me, that we wouldn't be able to communicate. Fortunately, that never happened.

Toward the end of his life, he couldn't move anything. He wasn't rigid; he just couldn't move on his own. At this point, he was in a hospital bed with nurses tending to him around the clock. Often I would go into his room early in the morning while it was still dark and crawl into bed with him. One morning, at about five o'clock, it was pitch dark when I walked toward the foot of his bed. I just stood there for a minute trying to see my way around, when suddenly I heard his voice saying, "Welcome." He never lost his incredible upbeat spirit throughout this terrible trying time. He never bemoaned his plight. He never said, "Why me?"

He also never discussed dying and did little to prepare for it. He had a will, but nothing else. But one night, about a month before he died, lying in his bed in the dark when I again walked into the room, he surprised me by saying, "You're beautiful and you're smart and you..." And then he said something else. But, I was so taken by what he had said—beautiful and smart—that I did not hear the rest of the sentence. That has driven me crazy ever since. I never knew what he was trying to tell me. This could have been his way of telling me that I would be able to manage without him, that I would be all right. I never heard those final words. I was too busy being flattered.

The day before Thanksgiving, November 24, 2009, around eleven in the morning, the doorbell rang. Standing in the doorway was a deliveryman with a huge bouquet of two dozen beautiful yellow roses. Inside was a note that said, "Happy Thanksgiving. Love, Abe." He had done it again. He always remembered special occasions: flowers, perfume, nightgowns, and birthday cakes in a hospital intensive care unit.

An hour later, Abe, Robert, and I were having a leisurely lunch on our sun porch. Robert had come to spend the day and we were having a light, fun time when Abe suddenly announced what he wanted for lunch the next day.

"I'd like to have a grilled ham and cheese sandwich tomorrow!"

Robert and I were laughing at this sudden statement, when all of a sudden, Abe turned his head in my direction, opened his eyes wide and looked straight at me. I was taken aback. He had not been able to turn his head or open his eyes for months.

"What's the matter, honey?" was my surprised question.

At this point, his head fell straight down on his chest and his eyes closed. He was dead.

CHAPTER EIGHT

For the first time in my life, I am now completely on my own. This doesn't mean I haven't done many things on my own (read: without my husband). The key word is "completely." This is an important difference. Whereas I built a psychotherapy practice, developed clinics, created a women's heart disease organization in twenty cities, traveled to China and India and around the U.S., I always had Abe at my back. I was never afraid to begin anything new or different "on my own" because I always felt his support, whether he agreed with me or not. He used to say to me, "Why do you ask me my advice when you're going to do what you want anyway?" My answer always was, "Yes, I will, but I still want to know what you think." I always valued his thoughtful answers even if I did the opposite. On my own, but always feeling his strength and good sense behind me.

Now, I talk to other people (I like to gather other people's thinking) and still often do the opposite, but I miss his calm strength. I am for the first time "completely" on my own.

Fortunately, I have enough confidence in my judgments, and I am thoughtful, careful, and thorough. I am still moving ahead with new ideas and projects, but I feel a gaping hole in my daily life: his reassuring voice. It hasn't deterred me from doing what I might plan; it is just as I am doing it, it feels empty. I think it's the lack of sharing the ups and downs, the thinking and planning, and the sense that I could always call on him. He was there most of my life. Now there is a giant empty space that can't be filled by anyone else.

My children are wonderful, there for me as I have needed them, but our shared experiences are different. They were there, for example, when we opened Capital Centre, but not in the room when we were fighting for a hockey franchise in Montreal.

It is up to me to get comfortable without my partner, get advice that I don't listen to, from others. Life moves on, whether you move with it or not. I was lucky to have such a person in my life.

This is the first time in my life that I must focus on me—what's good for me and what's not so good for me. From the time of my daughter's diagnosis with a congenital heart condition, until now, I have always had to be focused outward, on my children and my husband. It feels very strange, new and uncomfortable to think about *me*. I am not very good at it, but it is necessary if I hope to make the rest of my life as happy and fulfilling as it has been up to now.

Every day, I feel the sense of love I was fortunate to have, beginning with my grandparents, parents, sister, extended family, my children, and grandchildren. I treasure the sticky love notes my great-granddaughter leaves all over my house when she is here.

My hopes are that as time moves on, I will have less feelings of loneliness and more feelings of fulfillment.

Even as I have experienced terrible tragedy, watching my two children die, they also woke each morning with a smile. That is how I would like to greet each day.